RW

W9-BGF-070

3 2902 00034 1486

15.95

Getting Started in Powerboating

43030

797.125   Armstrong, Bob,
Arm   1937-

           Getting started
           in powerboating

NORTH INDIAN RIVER COUNTY LIBRARY
1001 C.R. 512
SEBASTIAN, FLORIDA 32958
PHONE (407) 589-1355

Getting Started In
POWERBOATING

Bob
Armstrong

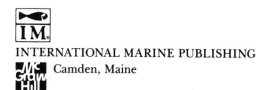

INTERNATIONAL MARINE PUBLISHING

Camden, Maine

43030

NORTH INDIAN RIVER COUNTY LIBRARY

Published by International Marine Publishing

10   9   8   7   6   5   4   3   2

Copyright © 1990 International Marine Publishing, an imprint of TAB
BOOKS. TAB BOOKS is a division of McGraw-Hill, Inc.

All rights reserved. The publisher takes no responsibility for the use of
any of the materials or methods described in this book, nor for the
products thereof. The name "International Marine" and the International
Marine logo are trademarks of TAB BOOKS. Printed in the United States
of America.

Library of Congress Cataloging-in-Publication Data

Armstrong, Bob, 1937–
    Getting started in powerboating / Bob Armstrong.
        p.   cm.
    ISBN 0-877-42-267-2
    1. Motorboats.   2. Boats and boating.   I. Title.
    GV835.A76   1990
    797.1'25–dc20   90-305514
                                                           CIP

TAB BOOKS offers software for sale. For information and a catalog,
please contact TAB Software Department, Blue Ridge Summit, PA
17294-0850.

Questions regarding the content of this book should be addressed to:

International Marine Publishing
P.O. Box 220
Camden, ME 04843

Printed by Fairfield Graphics, Fairfield, PA.
Design by Patrice M. Rossi.
Edited by Jon Eaton and Marty King.

CONTENTS

PREFACE   *ix*

PART 1

CHOOSING
THE
RIGHT BOAT

CHAPTER 1 No Boat Is Right for Everyone   *3*
2 Displacement Hulls   *12*
3 Planing Hulls   *24*
4 Semidisplacement Hulls   *37*
5 Comparing the Three Hull Types   *39*
6 Drive Systems   *50*
7 How to Read Boat Reviews and Tests   *61*
8 Twenty Questions to Codify Boat Selection   *65*

PART 2

THE WHYS OF
POWERBOAT
HANDLING

CHAPTER 9 Why Boats Don't Behave like Cars   *74*
10 The Twin-Screw Advantage   *79*
11 Transom Power   *83*
12 The Influence of the Wind   *88*
13 What Current Does   *93*

PART 3

THE HOWS OF
POWERBOAT
HANDLING

CHAPTER 14 Know Your Boat   *96*
15 Boathandling in Wind and Current   *99*
16 Docking a Single-Screw Inboard   *102*
17 The "Impossible" Moves with a Single-Screw Boat   *108*
18 Docking a Twin-Screw Inboard   *111*
19 Docking Transom-Powered Boats   *119*
20 Using Springlines for Maneuvering   *127*
21 Using Docklines   *137*
22 Anchors and Anchoring Techniques   *147*
23 Inlet Running   *165*
24 How to Handle Heavy Weather   *170*
25 Practice Makes Perfect   *178*

APPENDIX 1 Rules of the Road   *181*
APPENDIX 2 A Gallery of Powerboats   *187*
INDEX   *201*

Dedication

This book is dedicated to the memory of Joseph A. Savino.

September 20, 1920–April 28, 1989

For more than a dozen years I lived aboard, operated, and cared for his boats. Had he not been willing to let his captain be a writer as well, this book—and countless magazine articles—never could have happened. Had he not also given me the freedom to run other boats when the opportunities presented themselves, I would not have had the experience on which to base much of my writing. For these considerations, I thank him.

But more important, through all those years he was a true friend. For that, I will miss him.

R.J.A.

PREFACE

So you've been thinking about taking up the sport of powerboating? That's understandable: it looks like so much fun! But how do you start? If you're like many new boating people, your first step is to visit a nearby dealer or go to a boat show or two. Then suddenly you feel overwhelmed. What appeared to be so simple soon seems rather complicated. You quickly discover that there are more different kinds of boats than you'd ever imagined. You look around and realize you just don't know where to begin.

Well, powerboating *is* fun, and you'd probably have a pretty good time with any boat. But it's much *more* fun when you have the right boat and are comfortable handling it in just about any circumstance. That's why I've written this book. I'm in no better position to tell you exactly which boat is "right" for you than I am to choose the person you should marry, but I *can* offer practical suggestions for finding the boat of your dreams. Those suggestions are set forth in Part 1.

Parts 2 and 3 are designed to help you get off on the right foot when you begin to operate your new pride and joy. The boathandling and other operating tips I offer can make powerboating more fun by helping you to avoid many of the mistakes beginners usually make—mistakes that often spoil the great time you can have on the water.

There's no substitute for experience, but by taking advantage of someone else's experience, you can get off to a much happier start and make the learning process all the more pleasant. So dig in, read on, and get out on the water and enjoy!

PART

ONE

CHOOSING
THE
RIGHT BOAT

1 ◆ No Boat is Right for Everyone

To many people, the ideal powerboat would have a top speed somewhere approaching Mach 1 (or at least feel that way), have the living space of a penthouse condo, be as impressive as the Taj Mahal, operate on the budget of an economy car and never need maintenance. Of course it should also be comfortable at slow speeds for those times you're not in a hurry and should be small enough to make it easy to find room in the most crowded marina or anchorage.

But it should be big enough to allow you to bring along all your friends (when you have a boat, you have a lot of friends) yet not so big that you can't handle it yourself. It should also be large enough to make those open ocean passages you dream about (to faraway places with strange sounding names or just to the town on the other side of the bay) with fuel capacity to match. But then it shouldn't be so huge that you can't get close to shore when you reach your destination.

I think you get the picture: It would be nice to have a boat with all the features you could ever possibly want. Nice, but not possible. *Every boat is a compromise of sorts.* The laws of physics, hydrodynamics, aesthetics, economics, and other practical considerations force you to give up one thing to gain something else—in nearly every aspect of every situation. You simply cannot put ten pounds of coffee in a five-pound bag. So you have to decide what you want most and give up what you want least in order to have it.

If it's any consolation, this is the number-one rule of boat buying, and it applies to everyone. Even the ultrarich buyer of a custom-built megayacht has to live with trade-offs. That's right, even when its price is in the millions, no boat, no matter how large or luxurious, can have everything or be everything the owner might wish for. So I repeat boat-buying rule number one: Every boat is a compromise. Remember that, and you'll save yourself a lot of grief as you make choices to get the boat that's right for you.

We'll look more closely at the details of the choices as we go along. But for now, let's get our feet wet by exploring some generalities.

Size

We often tend to think that bigger is better. But when it comes to boats, it ain't necessarily so. Sure, bigger boats offer more amenities, the ability to carry more people, and greater fuel capacity (which usually, though not always, equates to greater range) and are often more comfortable than smaller boats when the going gets rough. But size should be a lesser consideration than many others. Because a basic truth of powerboating is that while you can have more *kinds* of fun in a larger boat, you can't have any *more* fun in a megayacht than you can in an outboard-powered dinghy. And sometimes you can only have less.

I say that with full acknowledgment that "How big is it?" will be one of the first questions people ask when they find out you have a boat. I also recognize that despite the many greater pleasures of owning a boat, being a "yachtsman" is often perceived as a status symbol. And the bigger the boat, the greater the perceived status. But being one who enjoys boating for boating's sake, I firmly believe that the goal should not be to have as much boat as you can afford, but rather to have no more boat than you can practically use.

Putting economic aspects aside (OK, no one buys a boat to save money, but we've come a long way from "If you have to ask how much it costs, you can't afford it," and you must face the truth that bigger boats not only cost more to buy, they cost more to maintain, operate, berth, insure, etc.—so the economics are important), there is another downside to bigger boats. They need more water! Not only in area—operating room, so to speak—but usually in depth as well. That means there are many places you can go in a small boat that are inaccessible to larger craft and places that give the operator of a small boat a wide margin of error while requiring a much greater degree of care and precision from the skipper of a large boat. So *where* you plan to go boating should have a strong influence on your decision as to how big a boat you need. (Where you go boating affects other decisions also. We'll get to them all in good time.)

Many years ago, I had a neighbor who learned the "size versus use" lesson the hard way. He had wanted a boat for years, and when he came into a moderate inheritance he finally could afford one, so he got it—a 26-foot inboard cabin cruiser with a flying bridge. It was a nice boat. Very nice. But not for him. You see, he wanted to use his boat not only on the ocean at our hometown's doorstep, but also on a nearby lake. So he kept his boat on a trailer for flexibility. But given the 11-foot tidal range in our native state of Maine, he could not launch or haul a boat this size at his convenience. To use the ramp on the estuary from which we gained access to the ocean, he had to wait for the right stage of tide—half flood or higher. So quite often the boat was stuck on land when he wanted it in the ocean, or in the estuary when he wanted to take it to the lake. Yes, his cruiser could sit on a trailer, but it was not really a trailerable boat. No wonder he traded it the following year for a 19-foot outboard runabout. The 19-footer was truly trailerable and suited his needs perfectly. And though I've suggested that larger boats can be more comfortable in heavy seas, I have to emphasize that this isn't always true either. I feel much more secure taking rough stuff in a 25-foot center-console fishing boat designed to go to sea than I do in a 60-footer that was designed to be a dockside "cocktail barge." So let's save the size question for later, when you have a better idea of all your needs.

Accommodations

"How many does it sleep?" will probably be the second most often asked question you get from acquaintances. And it can be an important consideration. But not yet. While it is true that today's family cruisers in the 26- to 30-foot range offer more amenities and comfort than most boats in the 36- to 40-foot range did 20 years ago, it is too soon to surmise that you need a cabin at all, much less a certain number of berths. Don't get me wrong, you may well end up with a family cruiser. Ever since the Electric Boat Company took yachting out of the exclusive grasp of the very rich and made boating a practical recreational outlet for everyone with the introduction of the ELCO Cruisette in 1915, the family cruiser has been the mainstay of popular boating. And I would have to agree with the consensus: There is probably no better all-around practical choice. But if accommodations—that is, places to sleep, a galley to cook in, a dedicated area for dining (even if it also converts to a sleeping area), and a head with a full shower—don't really figure in your boating plans, you don't need a cruiser. If your activities are by day only, perhaps a boat with more open deck area would be more suitable. Remember, a cabin takes up space. The more the amenities, the more space it takes. If those amenities are important, fine. But if they aren't, why pay for them and lose other features you might want more? Features such as a working cockpit for fishing, or room to stow scuba gear, or better access to the water for swimming, or more room simply to soak up the sun? Ultimately, how you plan to use your boat should dictate what it is. And that brings us to . . .

Activities

While it is true that you can fish from any boat, swim or dive from any boat, or take any boat cruising, not every boat allows you to conduct these activities with equal ease and comfort. So consider the number-two rule of boat buying: Your boat should make your favorite on-the-water activity easy. Of course, your boat will quite likely be a family boat, and the wishes of other family members should have influence also (which takes us back to rule one, compromise), so a pure fishing, or diving, or any other type of truly dedicated craft may be too highly specialized for all your needs. On the other hand, once you get to the 25-foot range, most boats offer a degree of convenient multiple use even if they can't be all things to all people. What you have to decide is which uses count most for you and your family.

You probably know the needs of your favorite on-the-water activity better than I do. But in the excitement of looking at new boats, you might forget. So let me run over a few of the most popular activities with a nod toward the boat features you'll need to enjoy them.

Fishing

Being a stable platform would probably top the list of fishboat features. All boats roll in a trough, but good fishing boats have an easy roll that doesn't go far enough or happen quickly enough to throw you off balance. When you check out a possible choice, be sure your sea trial includes seeing how the boat behaves at trolling speeds and sitting still in a seaway. If it isn't comfortable, keep looking.

Room for anglers to move around as they fight their catch would probably be the second biggest need. This means plenty of cockpit space, open deck room, or both. "Clean" space is important, too. That is, deck hardware—cleats, chocks, etc.—should be hidden or recessed so that anglers can't snag lines (or shins) while fighting their catch. And the cockpit or deck shouldn't be too far off the water.

You should also have rod holders, rod and tackle stowage, a bait prep center, perhaps outriggers for trolling, and an aerated well for holding live bait. The list of features should also include places to stow your catch and easy means of getting the catch aboard (which means a transom door in larger craft). Since fishing can be both wet and messy, the cockpit should be self-bailing and have facilities (pump, hose, etc.) for washdown underway. The area and its contents

Figure 1-1

THE COMPLETE ANGLER   *This Blackfin 38 is a fine example of a sportfisherman. Note the enclosed flying bridge, tower, outriggers, "rocket launchers," and efficient cockpit that includes a bait-prep center (port side, forward), rod holders in the covering boards, and a fighting chair. (Courtesy Blackfin Yachts)*

should also, by design, lend themselves to easy and frequent washdown; a fishing cockpit is not a place for the delicate or fancy—in either facilities or participants.

Low-speed maneuverability is also important unless you plan to fish "dead boat," which is impractical for trophy-sized catches. That generally means you'll want twin-screw power whether it's needed for any other reason or not. Often it will be needed simply to provide more total horsepower, because it's a given that the best fishing areas are not always close to the best living areas. Hence, many anglers want a boat that will get to the fish and back in a hurry. That usually means plenty of horsepower. Visibility from the helm is also critical. On larger boats the console is often elevated with a flying bridge to provide a higher vantage point for better all-around visibility. In many regions (south Florida, for one) a tower is added to raise the observation point even higher. In large boats the main station may be so far from the action that a separate console is needed in the cockpit.

Of course, many of these features are options you can add to any boat anytime. But you should consider them from the start or it may be too difficult (or expensive) to include them later.

Swimming and Diving

If all you wear is a bathing suit (or less), all you really need for the activity is a boarding ladder—an easy way to get back aboard from the water. But if you add flippers, mask and snorkel, air tank and regulator, weights, wet suit and other scuba paraphernalia, ease of getting into the water becomes as important as ease of getting out.

Room to move around near the boarding area is important, too, so cockpit space can be as valuable for swim/dive boats as it is for fishing boats. The only difference is that the cockpit sole can be higher off the water as long as the ladder is adequate. This is especially true if the boat has a transom platform. Often called a swim platform, this feature gives you a place to don or remove gear just inches from the water and is an unbeatable addition to any boat used for extensive in-the-water activities. A freshwater shower on or near the platform is a nice plus, too, even if you do your swimming in fresh water. The shower is usually cleaner, often warmer, and will probably feel good afterward no matter where you swim.

While it is not a consideration for swimming or even snorkeling, space to stow scuba gear becomes important if you plan to do much serious diving. It's amazing how much room even the most elementary gear requires—and how aggravating it can be if there's no proper place to put it. Racks for air tanks are particularly desirable, because loose tanks on a pitching deck can become dangerous unguided missiles. Proper stowage also leads to longer equipment life and should be a very big consideration if diving is high on your list.

Ground tackle—anchors, rode, and the facilities for handling them—is important on every boat, but particularly so for swimming and diving. Arrangements that would be acceptable on other boats can prove totally inadequate when frequent anchoring is routine. A windlass or "automatic" anchor handling system is not a luxury on a dive boat, it's nearly a must.

Cruising

Many years ago I did some extensive traveling in a 19-foot open runabout. No head, no galley, no berths. I must also add, no comfort. It was strictly roughing it all the way. It was fun, but I was younger then, and the adventure was part of it. Today, I want a good mattress under me when I sleep, a fully equipped galley with freezer and microwave when I get hungry, a shower with hot water to help me feel fully "civilized," and TV with VCR to indulge my fantasies. I won't leave home without 'em. These days I live aboard a large motoryacht as a professional captain and never leave home at all. I take it with me wherever I go.

How you go is up to you. Some folks approach cruising simply as travel on water as opposed to travel on land. That is, they consider accommodations as part of the destination package and cruise from one resort complex (complete with shoreside motel) to another. If you feel that way, just about any boat will work. But most cruising folk think as I do—they don't want to be limited to destinations with shoreside accommodations, and take home along. This means having a boat with a cabin, sufficient berths for your crew, a proper galley and dining area, at least one head with shower, and enough total space to prevent cabin fever over a reasonable length of cruise. When you travel this way, your destinations are nearly unlimited.

Adequate space can be particularly sensitive because privacy is a fragile thing aboard most cruising boats. I steadfastly believe that anyone who needs too much privacy is a poor cruising companion, but we all need our personal space, and the longer we stay in a confined area (and even megayachts become confined after a time), the more important it is. So give consideration to the space *arrangement* as well as total volume.

Since many areas serve double duty—convertible dinettes are a perfect example—the number of available berths is usually greater than the number of people a boat can truly accommodate. So, "How many does it sleep?" is still a lesser consideration. Stowage—for clothing, personal belongings, food, and other necessities—is perhaps more important. Its importance grows with the length of the cruise. A boat that might suit six overnight could become cramped for one couple after a week if there isn't room for the gear, provisions, and personal effects you need to feel comfortable and happy over a period of time.

Speed and range are factors to consider in all boats, but they are particularly important to cruising boats because of the influence they have on your overall activity. The two are not necessarily mutually exclusive, but as we'll discover later on, either factor can impose severe limitations on the other. If most of your cruising will be done on weekends, speed can perhaps be more important. If getting away from it all for longer periods is more to your liking, you should probably opt for range.

Waterskiing

While you can ski behind any boat with enough power to pull the skiers and enough speed to make it fun, the best ski boats are small, fast, and highly maneuverable, with a small turning radius and a flat wake. The tow rope should attach to a pylon somewhere near the boat's pivot point. Since this combination of features is not always desirable for many other activities, waterskiing is perhaps the one sport that begs a truly dedicated craft. Because the best ski boats tend to be smaller, however, it is often not at all impractical to have a ski boat in addition to a larger, more general-purpose family boat if a variety of activities is desired.

Partying

Yes, a few pages back I did say I'd rather take rough stuff in a boat designed for it than in a cocktail barge. But I didn't intend to disparage either the idea of having parties onboard or the boats designed to have them. Rather, I mean to make the point that this too is a factor to be considered in the trade-offs.

Celebrating afloat has a special charm that few parties ashore can match. It's a super way to repay social obligations. As one megayacht owner put it, "People who might not attend a party at my house never refuse an invitation to my boat." The principle applies even if your boat is considerably smaller than a megayacht.

Of course, size *is* a factor if only to the extent that available space determines how large a party you can throw. But as it is with cruising, the way space is arranged is more important, except that for partying the emphasis is perhaps less on places to put things away and more on places to put things out. Likewise, there is less concern for privacy and more for open space and traffic flow. A balance of space is nice, too; the best party setups include both enclosed saloons and open deck areas.

Such amenities as wet bar, icemaker(s), and liquor and glass storage are nice, but not necessary. Their importance varies in direct proportion to total available space and their compatibility with other uses of the boat.

For pure partying, a cocktail barge does not need to be terribly seakindly, since some of the best parties don't require leaving the pier. If you do take a cruise, it will most likely be a short one over protected water in nice weather. Otherwise, the party is no fun. Of course, if you have other uses in mind, their needs must be considered also, and the boat must provide for them as well. (Compromise, remember?)

Since drinking and operating a boat are as bad a combination as drinking and driving, I'd also advise owner/skippers to hire a pro to run the boat for them while they party. This also lets you enjoy the party as host instead of being preoccupied as boat operator, so it's not a bad idea even if you don't drink. Both are excellent reasons for having a full-time professional captain on a truly dedicated party boat.

Other Considerations

Speed

This is a relative concept. A trawler yacht ambling along at 10 knots seems fast to the people in a 6-knot sailboat, yet the 30- to 40-knot speeds now quite common in modern family cruisers are slow to those in the 70 mph (or faster) raceboat-derived "performance" craft. The bottom line, however, is that speed on the water is a result of three factors: 1) horsepower, 2) weight, and 3) shape. The faster you want to go, the more you have to increase 1, decrease 2, and streamline 3. Since we are, at this point, still just getting our feet wet, we'll save the details for subsequent chapters. But for the moment let's note that increasing horsepower generally means using bigger engines, which need more room and burn more fuel. Since bigger engines usually weigh more and their greater fuel demand necessitates a concomitant greater fuel capacity, increasing horsepower will likely increase total weight far beyond the weight of the engines themselves.

Modern construction techniques and materials—including cored laminates, unidirectional fabrics, improved resins, and hollow stringers reinforced with carbon fiber—have done a lot to reduce the weight of the hull and superstructure while maintaining (or often even increasing) strength. But when you add bigger engines and greater fuel capacity, it usually works out that other things, such as amenities, have to give way to keep total weight down, and of course, the sleeker the boat, the less room there is likely to be inside. That, too, can limit amenities. So the real bottom line is that despite technological advances that have made great strides in allowing boats to have speed and other goodies as well, speed is usually but one more item to be traded off against other desires and needs.

Range

This is simply the amount of available fuel (usually on the order of 90 percent of total fuel carried) divided by consumption (gallons per hour) times speed (miles per hour or knots as the situation requires) at a given throttle setting. The answer will be a distance in statute miles for mph and nautical miles for knots. Deduct another 10 percent to be conservative and you'll know how far you can go at that speed.

While it might seem that the more fuel you carry, the farther you can travel, this too is not always so. What is true is that the less fuel you burn, the farther you can go, which usually means that range is gained at a sacrifice of speed. Even ultrafast megayachts with fuel capacity measured in the thousands of gallons must throttle back to gain transatlantic range.

The reason increased capacity alone won't guarantee increased range is that added fuel is added weight. So unless other factors are also changed, the additional fuel is often consumed merely in carrying itself. Most production boats are designed to carry the optimum quantity of fuel for their normal cruise speed, and when it comes to range, what you get is what you've got. It is possible to increase a boat's range beyond that of its initial design, but to do so usually entails more engineering than simply adding tankage.

Comfort

This is another factor highly influenced by where you do your boating. In south Florida, totally open boats are fine, the main concern being a Bimini top or other protection from the sun. Indeed, boats intended for use in this area don't need an inside control station even if they have a cabin. If they do have a cabin, air conditioning is a must.

In New England and around Great Lakes country, dual stations are common; a flying bridge console is fine, weather permitting, but a more protected station is needed too often to do without. In the Pacific Northwest, protection from the weather is needed so constantly that outside controls were rare until the area's builders began marketing their craft elsewhere.

Comfort is definitely a "when in Rome" situation, and you'll find there's a good reason why the majority of boats in your area are arranged and equipped as they are. Deviate at your own risk.

Seaworthiness

"As much as possible" might be your initial reaction, but the truth is that this factor, too, should be dictated by how and where you use your boat. If you only plan to putter around Lake Calmandserene in good weather, you don't need the

Figure 1-2

HELM PROTECTION *The hard top over the flying bridge of this Viking 38 will fend off the sun. A canvas Bimini top offers similar protection and can be folded out of the way when not needed. In either case, plastic side curtains add protection from wind and rain. (Courtesy Viking Yachts)*

Figure 1-3

FLOATING HOME *Houseboats, such as this Harbormaster 375, combine the spaciousness of a cottage with the ability to travel. Generally designed for use on the protected waters of lakes, bays, and rivers, they provide far more living space than you'll find in sleeker craft.*

same kind of boat you would use for serious ocean tournament fishing. The large cabin windows you'd find so desirable for cruising along protected waterways (because they allow better sightseeing and minimize cabin fever) could be downright dangerous for offshore passagemaking. Most other factors that increase seaworthiness are also gained at the loss of something you would find quite nice under less stringent conditions. Being realistic in your estimate of how you plan to use your boat is as important in this matter as it is in others. Believe it or not, you can have too much seaworthiness. The extra beef built into offshore boats is not without cost. Given that we all have a practical limit to the cost of the boat we get, if you don't need the beef, your money can go toward things you want more.

The goal is to match your boat to your needs, not to some preconceived, hypothetical "best." There is no one boat that's right for everyone, but there is a boat that's right for you. In subsequent chapters, we'll look at more details that will help you to find it.

———————◆———————

2. Displacement Hulls

So far, we've looked mostly at features built onto or into the boat. Now it's time to take a close look at the boat itself. The one thing that makes a cabin cruiser different from an RV, a runabout different from a sports car, is the hull— the part that goes in the water. In this chapter we'll look at *displacement* hulls, despite the truth that in the pleasureboating of the early 1990s, they are a decided minority. Displacement is where it all begins.

How Does a Boat Float?

As Archimedes discovered back in ancient Greece, the weight of an object is equal to the weight of the water it displaces. Boats and other things that float do so because their volume, the space they occupy, is greater than the volume of water they displace.

Let's say you have a boat that weighs 5 tons, an even 10,000 pounds, fully loaded (that is, including engines, fuel, stores, gear, and people aboard). Then let's say we have a tank large enough to hold your boat. If you were to fill that tank to the brim and then set your boat in it, you would find (let's say you have a way to do this, also) that the water which would spill out of the tank when you set your boat in—the water *displaced*—would also weigh exactly 5 tons.

But putting that 10,000 pounds of water into the mold from which the hull was produced would nowhere near fill it. In fact, though it's not so surprising when you think about it, the water would come up to the point in the mold where you'd find the load waterline on the hull itself.

All of this is in illustration of the neat fact of life that allows us to use materials that don't float—steel, aluminum, or fiberglass-reinforced plastic (FRP), for example—to build boats that do. We simply have to form the material into a shape that has a greater volume than the water it displaces. A boat needs to do more than just stay afloat, however, and the shape of the hull also has a great influence on its performance and stability.

Performance and stability are important considerations. They, too, are among the trade-offs you have to make in choosing a boat, and each hull type offers its own interpretation of both factors.

Of course we have to note that all hulls are in a displacement mode at rest. It's when we get underway that the differences show up. In the next chapter, we'll look at boats that can get up on top of the water when they run fast enough. But for now we'll continue to examine hulls that remain *in* the water—the displacement mode—at all times, even at wide-open throttle.

Performance

Every coin has two sides. The downside of displacement hulls is that they are relatively slow—generally doing 12 knots or less in the size range of popular powerboating. The upside is that they can achieve this speed with little applied horsepower. Indeed, though some skippers will choose twin screws for easier maneuvering and other supposed advantages, many displacement hulls run quite nicely with but a single small engine. Needing little horsepower means operating with relatively low fuel consumption, which equates either to smaller fuel tanks and more space for accommodations, or greater range with larger tankage.

Since you don't have to concern yourself with getting up on top of the water, you can generally be less concerned about the total weight of a displacement boat. In fact, increasing a displacement hull's load can actually increase its speed. The plus to this is that you can fill a displacement boat with all kinds of goodies—more amenities, more fuel, more water, more stowage, etc.—and not only avoid a penalty but in many cases derive a benefit. And that's only true for displacement hulls.

Stability

Displacement hulls are usually very seakindly. High-speed hulls may be seakindly at cruising speeds but often do not perform comfortably at displacement speeds (though there are some that work well at nearly all throttle settings). Displacement hulls, on the other hand, can usually maintain their cruising speed (slow though it may be) under a greater variety of conditions, including snotty weather that would make running at high speed downright uncomfortable if not totally impossible. Some displacement hulls roll more than most folks like, particularly in beam seas. But (as we'll discover in due time), this is only a matter of comfort, as the rolling is an inherent part of the vessel's true stability. It can also be easily corrected with mechanical antiroll systems, and fortunately not all displacement hulls are equally guilty. Then, too, I can't think of anything that rolls more than some planing hulls do when they're not on plane, since they achieve stability solely through a hydrodynamic action that is missing unless they are moving fast.

Figure 2-1

TRAWLER YACHTS   *Trawler-type boats such as this Grand Banks 46 can usually handle heavy seas that are a problem for lighter varieties.*

Having made these sweeping statements, it's now time to add some background as to why they are so. I hope you find the following information interesting in its own right, as detail to further your appreciation of boats and their behavior. But alas, I'm afraid you'll also find some of it necessary simply to trigger the ever-important "But wait a minute, what about . . . ?" question you'll have to raise from time to time when an enthusiastic salesman carries exaggeration too far. Though the boating industry is perhaps better than some in its percentage of knowledgeable salespeople (no doubt brought about by the number of people who come into the business because they like boats in the first place), there are still those who hardly know the pointy end from the transom. So if *you* don't know why boats behave as they do, you could end up buying a bill of goods instead of the boat you want.

Displacement Speeds—a Closer Look

Every displacement boat has what is commonly called its "hull speed." Unfortunately, "hull speed" is one of the most bandied about yet least understood terms in boating. As applied to displacement hulls, it might be defined simply as the maximum speed attainable without applying ridiculous horsepower. Because *any* hull will plane if you push it hard enough.

To put hull speed in a real world perspective, let's see how it relates to you and the throttle lever. Say it takes 200 hp to push your boat as fast as it will go in a displacement mode. Yet let's also say the builder has given you 250 hp to play with. Once you throttle up to the 200 hp point on the power curve, you're going as fast as you can. Push the throttle all the way and you'll only burn more fuel and make more noise. The "extra" 50 hp gives you better economy (a 250 hp engine putting out 200 is more fuel efficient than a 200 hp engine working at maximum load), longer engine life (for similar reasons), and some added thrust when you need it for maneuvering. But it won't make you go any faster. It could take 800 hp or *more* (depending on how closely the hull shape approaches a planing design and how much the boat weighs) to make that boat go faster than "hull speed."

The reasons for this speed limit lie in the way a displacement hull moves *through* the water. It makes waves. Can't help it. And waves are bound by immutable laws of physics. Put a boat into a wave system and, not so strangely, its behavior will be strongly influenced by the same laws. But notice I said strongly, not totally.

This is not to suggest that boats are not also bound by laws of physics. Of course they are. In fact, by the time you finish this book you will have seen many ways in which boats are virtually living physics labs. My point is that the laws regarding free-wave motion are not the only laws influencing boat behavior. If they were, there would be far less variety in displacement hull performance.

Speed Relates to Length

Open-water wave systems move along at a speed-to-length ratio of 1.34. This means that you can determine the speed of advance of waves by measuring the distance between crests (wave length) and multiplying the square root of the wave length by 1.34. This is one of the immutable laws. Since displacement hulls often attain their greatest speed when they generate a wave whose length equals the waterline length of the boat, it has been assumed (and too often stated as gospel) that the hull speed of a displacement boat *must be* 1.34 times the square root of its waterline length. This is *not* immutable.

The truth is that a displacement hull will achieve a maximum speed-to-length ratio of 1.34 more easily than higher speeds. It's always easier to work *with* nature. It's certainly possible and even common for displacement hulls to be designed and powered for speed-to-length ratios higher than 1.34, but horse-power needs increase geometrically with speed at these high ratios.

It should be obvious that shape is involved also. Wedges, needles, nails, and other pointy objects penetrate solids more easily than do blunt objects. The bows of boats are tapered for similar reasons: It's easier to cut the water than to plow through it. Similarly, the way a boat *leaves* the stern wave is important, too, so the shape of the boat at the stern has influence as well. Indeed, breaking away from the tough grasp of the stern wave is one of the challenges of attaining a speed-to-length ratio greater than 1.34.

The *shape* of the boat in the water is as significant in many ways as the *length* of the boat in the water, and hull efficiency comes into play for displacement

Figure 2-2

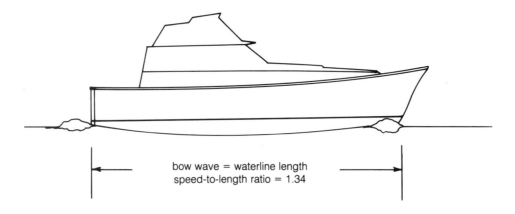

bow wave = waterline length
speed-to-length ratio = 1.34

SPEED-TO-LENGTH RATIO *When a boat's bow wave equals its waterline length, its speed-to-length ratio is 1.34. Given enough power, displacement hulls can achieve a speed-to-length ratio of up to 2.0.*

Figure 2-3

STO. DOMINGO EXPRESS

SHAPE AFFECTS SPEED *Though it does not relate directly to pleasureboats, the bulbous bow often seen below the waterline on ships is a perfect illustration of one way in which hull shape influences speed. Without this protrusion, the ship would be slower.*

hulls fully as much (though in different ways) as we'll soon find out it does for planing hulls.

To give other arguments their due, some say that any speed-to-length ratio higher than 1.34 puts the boat into the "semidisplacement" category (we'll discuss the nature of this beast a couple of chapters later). However, many naval architects agree that speed-to-length ratios up to 2.0 may still be considered displacement hulls. Ratios between 2.0 and 4.0 are likely to belong to semidisplacement hulls, and any boat with a ratio over 4.0 will undoubtedly be planing.

To further refute the "must be 1.34" element, I offer as proof the boat I am sitting on as I write these words. It is steel, nearly 80 feet overall, with a 25-foot beam and a 6-foot draft. It weighs about 160 tons fully loaded. Definitely a displacement hull! But it was designed to achieve a hull speed of 13 knots, and by golly it can. With 70 feet on the waterline (square root 8.37), this equates to a speed-to-length ratio of 1.55.

Granted, it takes every bit of the 750 horses aboard to get the 13 knots. But 800, 1000, or even 1500 hp would push it no faster. Yet throttling back to 400 hp still gives us 10 knots and much better efficiency (about half the fuel it takes to produce 750 hp). If 1.34 were always the magic number, this boat would top out at 11.2 knots no matter what.

As a side note just to show how complex it all can be, a naval architect working on big ship design once told me about having to modify the computer program used to analyze the results of tank-testing hull models. The reason: There proved to be a slight but measurable difference in performance between hulls *pulled* through the water by external forces (as are the test models), and those *pushed* through by the action of their own propellers (as happens in the real world). You can't take any of it for granted.

Speed Also Relates to Power

Let's look at three similar displacement hulls, all of them "trawler" yachts with an overall length in the upper thirties and a waterline length of 32 feet. The square root of 32 is 5.66, so if boat A has a speed-to-length ratio of 1.34, its maximum displacement speed will be about 7½ knots (1.34 X 5.66). If boat B has a speed-to-length ratio of 1.55, we have a nearly 9-knot boat (8.8), and if boat C's S/L ratio is 2.0, the generally considered cut-off for pure displacement performance, we have a boat that can do slightly better than 11 knots.

Here's where the trade-offs come in. While the waterline lengths are identical, their speed-to-length ratios are different, so their maximum speeds are different. That means their power requirements are different, too—but only to exceed 7½ knots. It would take roughly the same horsepower to match speeds to that point in all three boats. The difference is that boats B and C will need more power to be able to reach their full potential. A lot more. If 112 hp is enough to get the 7½ knots, boat A can be equipped with a single 125 hp diesel and do quite nicely—you'd have the reserve we discussed above. But boat C would probably need a minimum of 250 hp to get its 11 knots, which would mean either a larger single engine or two of the same engines used in boat A. Either way, boat C will inevitably cost more to buy.

The Options

We won't yet worry about the debate between singles and twins—we'll leave that to a later chapter. For now we'll just say the boats are much alike except that A has 125 hp in the engine compartment and C has 250. Let's make everything else—the accommodations plans, fuel capacities, and such—identical. Given the same amount of fuel, at 7½ knots both boats would have a nearly identical range. For ease of figuring, let's make it 500 miles. On this basis, boat C's range would drop to about 330 miles if you throttled up to 11 knots. Please note that these figures are for comparison in broad terms. As it says on the car window stickers, actual mileage may vary.

If it's 50 miles between Bon Voyage and Lazzez le Bon Temps Roulet, the trip will take 6 hours and 40 minutes at 7½ knots, but only 4½ hours at 11. Not too big a difference. But if the distance between ports is 100 miles, you're looking at nearly 13½ hours on the water in boat A, versus about 9 hours in boat C—a big difference when you consider daylight hours, activities on arrival, the availability of dock help, fuel dock hours, and other related factors affecting both departure and arrival times.

But you must also remember that in getting there faster, boat C burns about 1.5 times as much fuel as boat A. So it not only costs more to buy, it costs more to run.

To complete the comparison, boat B would need about 160 hp to get its near 9 knots. Under the same guidelines as above, it would have a range of about 419 miles and would make a 50-mile trip in just over 5½ hours, burning about 1.2 times the fuel of boat A. Of course, boat C throttled back to 9 knots would do about the same.

The one constant in all this is the waterline length. Increase that and you increase hull speed no matter what the S/L ratio—longer boats can go faster. Loading a displacement hull so it sits deeper in the water also effectively adds to the waterline length. That's why displacement hulls are used for load-carrying workboats and another reason why they are so loved for long-range cruising. You can bring aboard all the fuel, supplies, and comforts you need and gain speed (however slightly) in the process.

Stability . . . Again (in Greater Detail)

Stability might be defined as a boat's ability to remain upright—no matter what. This might seem an oversimplification, yet it is really what we are primarily after: a boat that won't turn turtle. Period. Of course we complicate things by wanting to feel comfortable at the same time. And given that pleasureboats operate over a wide set of conditions regarding load, trim, and operator skill, we also want a boat that will remain stable without much thought or work on our part.

Our main concern is transverse (side-to-side) stability. Longitudinal (fore-and-aft) stability is less of a problem, though boats with less than ideal longitudinal stability often give a wet ride. But it is rolling that really bothers us. It can be uncomfortable and, carried to the extreme, can lead to capsizing.

Fortunately, today's pleasureboats are generally very stable, and unless we do a truly horrendous job of improper loading or take the boat into much heavier seas than it was designed for, we don't have to worry about capsizing. Comfort, however, is another story. As we'll see, a certain amount of rolling motion is inherent in a stable hull. But that doesn't make it feel any better. So we often use antiroll devices—also called "stabilizers"—to make the ride smoother. But before we can fully appreciate what stabilizers do, we have to understand stability as it exists without them.

Stability, like a lot of other things in nature, results from a balance of forces, which tends to keep the boat upright (static stability) or, more important to our scheme of things, return it to upright when external forces disturb it (dynamic stability). Many of these forces have been observed, though perhaps not understood, since the first clever caveman carved a canoe.

Chances are our earliest ancestral boatmen merely hitched a ride on a floating log and so discovered buoyancy. The first person who came up with the idea to cut into the log and make a dugout got a vessel that was not only better for carrying things but also more stable; cutting away part of the log lowered its center of gravity. When some distant relatives added outriggers for even greater stability, they discovered the positive effects of beam.

In Figure 2-4 we see the forces of stability diagrammed. The center of gravity (G) is the hypothetical point at which an object's weight appears to be concentrated. A boat floats because this downward force is balanced by the upward force of buoyancy. As with gravity, we can assume a point (B) where all the buoyancy appears to be concentrated.

Figure 2-4

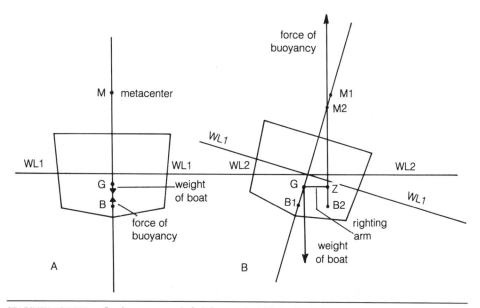

STABILITY FORCES *In A, metacentric height equals GM. In B, it has grown shorter and now equals GM_2. As the boat rolls, the righting arm GZ develops to return the hull to an even keel. In his effort to enhance stability, the designer will try to increase the magnitude of both GM and GZ in the rolling hull.*

In normal trim, these forces are in direct opposition—B is below G. This is static stability. When the boat rolls, even a little, we are looking at dynamic stability. When the hull lists, B moves toward the lower side, and a vertical line drawn upward from B cuts the vertical centerline at a point we call the metacenter (M). A boat's initial metacenter is determined when we roll the boat an infinitesimal, almost unmeasurable, amount.

Generally speaking, G does not move when the boat rolls. However, B and M do. The distance from the center of gravity to the metacenter, known as metacentric height (GM), decreases as M moves down the vertical centerline.

Metacentric height is, to a degree, a measure of a boat's stability. The greater the GM, the stiffer the hull; that is, the less its tendency to roll. We don't want a boat to be too stiff, however, because in its own way a stiff vessel can be as uncomfortable as one that rolls too much, and potentially dangerous to boot. No matter how stiff the boat, an angry sea can throw it off an even keel; when that happens, the same design characteristics that make the boat stiff to begin with may also make it slow to recover its footing once heeled. The designer must ensure that the boat's shape and weight distribution create adequate *righting moment* to return the boat to an even keel. The righting moment is a force resulting from buoyancy working on the righting arm, and a boat with healthy righting moment will roll—at least until we add antiroll devices.

In Figure 2-4(b) we see that a righting arm (GZ) develops as the boat heels or lists. At some point, the righting arm will have sufficient leverage to push the hull back upright. Then, of course, it will roll to the other side until another righting arm develops the moment to bring it back.

Though constant rolling may be uncomfortable, it does indicate a healthily functioning system: The boat's righting moment is not letting it roll too far to either side. In this sense, perhaps, rolling is to stability as bending is to the longevity of a twig. A twig that bends can survive the strongest winds, while a stiff one may snap if the pressure becomes too great. To put it another way, *returning* to an even keel is more important than *staying* on an even keel.

The righting moment is essentially a matter of leverage, and so the resulting force can be made stronger either by pushing harder or by using a longer lever. In this case our lever is the righting arm GZ. We have already seen that the righting arm increases as the boat rolls. But since we want to achieve stability without excessive roll, we often seek other ways to get the same result. Our choices are to make the righting arm longer by either lowering the center of gravity or increasing beam (which essentially moves B farther from the centerline as the boat rolls), or to increase the force of buoyancy. Since buoyancy is largely related to hull shape, it is possible to have a shape in which the force of buoyancy increases as the hull lays over. The result is again a greater righting moment produced from a lesser angle of roll. Truly comfortable hulls generally use all three elements in varying proportions, and a wide, low boat with a lot of reserve buoyancy will be very seakindly indeed.

Obviously, one way to have a lower center of gravity is to give the boat a relatively deep draft—the more boat in the water compared with what's above the waterline, the more stable the boat. But deep draft and pleasureboating do not truly go hand in hand because many pleasureboat destinations can't take deep draft vessels. But draft, per se, is not the objective; balance is.

Achieving the right balance for good stability is a problem faced by naval architects no matter what type of hull we're discussing. But since displacement hulls are often derived from traditional workboat lines—in the "trawler" yacht (see Figure 2-1), we've even borrowed the name of the North Sea fishing boats on which they are based—the differences between the original and the derivation raise additional problems. For example, real trawlers are designed not only to go after fish, but also to bring home the catch—*tons* at a time. Eliminate the payload and the boat doesn't sit or ride properly. And even if the trawler yacht were to have the same lines as a working trawler and a load of ballast to make her sit on her lines, the result would not be practical for pleasureboating. She'd carry way too much draft and require more boathandling skill than most amateur boatmen would have.

So most pleasureboat displacement hulls, regardless of what they are called, are at best *modifications* of workboat designs and thus must be cursed with a higher center of gravity. This is not to say that such boats are topheavy but rather that they will very likely have a less comfortable roll than the commercial craft they resemble, and some very salty-looking craft prove to be a lot less comfortable than you would imagine from their appearance.

One more note on shape. Since it is common dockside knowledge that "round-bottomed boats roll more," I think it is only right to clarify things. The statement is true without question if we are talking about a hull shape in which the whole bottom is rounded. In fact, the more closely the hull shape resembles an arc of a circle, the more roll we'll have. But a hull with round (soft) bilges will not roll appreciably more than a hard-chined hull if the lines are otherwise basically the same.

Motion Minders

Antiroll devices come in two forms, passive and active, as described by the way they work their magic. As the appellations suggest, passive antiroll devices just hang there, while active devices do something positive.

Figure 2-5

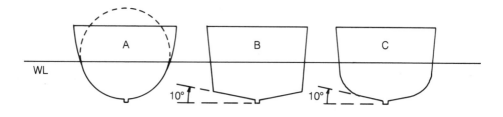

ROLLING VERSUS HULL SHAPE   *Hull A will roll easily because its shape is nearly circular. Hulls B and C will both roll less than A. Hull C will roll no more than B despite its rounded bilges, because both have 10-degree-deadrise shallow-V bottoms of equal beam and draft.*

Among the most popular passive devices are *flopper stoppers* for at-rest situations and *paravanes* for use underway. Flopper stoppers may be hung just about any way, but paravanes are hung overboard from booms. The vanes add to the vessel's rolling inertia and tend to reduce uncomfortable motion simply by making it physically harder to produce a roll in either direction. That the vanes must be set and retrieved as conditions require (for example, they are in the way coming into a marina) is but one of their drawbacks. Another is that they don't work as effectively as active devices. On the plus side, they *do* work; being relatively simple they are less expensive than active devices, and because they are "mechanical" only in the simplest sense and have no sophisticated parts nor need for electric power, they will continue to work, free of breakdown, with little maintenance. The need for booms and masts from which to suspend the booms does limit their use to boats which have room for such arrangements, but then again, this category includes many types of displacement craft.

There are several types of active antiroll devices, including such things as weights on tracks that slide hydraulically in the opposite direction whenever a roll begins. But by far the most common are fin-type stabilizers, which control the rolling of a boat in much the same way that ailerons on an airplane wing cause the plane to bank in turns. Using a gyroscope to sense the slightest deviation from upright, the system angles the fins to produce an immediate counter-roll. Be-

Figure 2-6

STABILIZER, VERSION 1   *This paravane is a* passive *stabilizer, and in use would be hung over the side on a cable suspended from a boom. The cylindrical weight forces the paravane underwater, while the horizontal "wing" tends to resist lift and keep it there. With one of these devices hanging off each side of a boat, its tendency to roll is greatly reduced. (Courtesy Atlantic & Gulf Fishing Supply Corp.)*

cause the hull doesn't have to use its designed-in righting moment (which would eventually develop, but not until the boat had rolled farther), the difference in comfort level is almost unbelievable. Of course, no device can completely eliminate rolling, but a good fin system can go a long way toward that objective.

I should also add that there are only a few choices in the marketplace of stabilizer systems. Each manufacturer offers a good product, and all have survived an era in which the incompetent have been weeded out. Since the integrity of installation is more important than the make of the system, you should pay more attention to installing correctly sized fins in the correct locations than to selecting a brand. With a new boat, simply have the builder install the system as a part of initial construction. If you are retrofitting, make sure the yard knows what it is doing. In either case, going with system types and sizes they have used successfully in the past should produce like results for you.

A final note regarding the positive effects of active stabilization. In addition to enhancing comfort, a properly installed system can also increase fuel efficiency and, particularly in displacement boats, even add to your speed. They do this despite the inevitable drag the fins create because a boat that rolls less will usually run a straighter track. That translates to a better speed made good—you spend less time wandering, and that, of course, means you burn less fuel.

A well-balanced, stable displacement boat can take you nearly anywhere because it will make its speed no matter what, and given the lack of weight

Figure 2-7

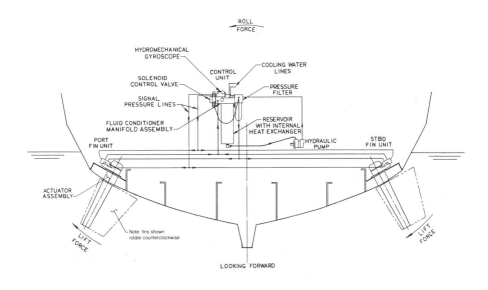

STABILIZER, VERSION 2   *This is an example of an active stabilizing system. Working similarly to the ailerons on a plane, the fins can actually make a boat roll to either side, much as an airplane banks. A gyroscope senses true vertical and directs the fins to produce a counter-roll opposing the natural roll induced by the hull's reaction to wave motion. The result is near-level cruising. (Courtesy Naiad Stabilizers)*

restrictions (both statements must be prefaced by "within reason"), you can also go in considerable comfort. All of which is a pretty strong argument in favor of displacement hulls. But still, to a lot of people, displacement boats are no good because "they can't get out of their own way." So in the next chapter, we'll look at boats that *can!*

———————◆———————

3 ◆ Planing Hulls

Displacement hulls, while desirable for many purposes, just don't go fast enough for most modern recreational boatmen. It seems we're in a hurry to relax. That's why the majority of today's pleasure craft are designed to plane—to get up and move across the water rather than through it. There are many approaches to the task of making a boat get up and go, and in this chapter we'll cover some of the advantages and disadvantages of each. Though by now it shouldn't be a surprise, there are trade-offs to be made in the choice of hull form even within the category of planing hulls.

As I pointed out in the last chapter, any hull can plane if you apply enough power. One of the objectives in designing a planing boat, however, is to get the boat on plane with as little horsepower as possible. Granted, the power required for a planing hull will always be greater than that needed by a displacement boat of similar size, but it is nowhere near that which would be necessary to plane a hull not designed for the purpose. However, just as we ask of all hulls that they do more than simply stay afloat, we also ask that planing hulls do more than simply plane. We often sacrifice a degree of planing efficiency in an effort to gain other attributes.

Deep-V, Modified-V, and Other Arcane Shapes

As Figure 3-1 shows, a flat surface will plane with little difficulty—even if it isn't a boat! The photo is from the early 1950s. In those days, my father, who knew this fact well and gave me much of my basic boating education, constantly amazed (and often embarrassed) the owners of sleeker, supposedly faster boats by racing them in a tubby, flat-bottomed, solid wood skiff powered by a 5-horse outboard kicker. He'd just lock down the tiller so he didn't have to sit back by the motor and move his considerable weight forward until the boat reached optimum trim, and then he'd let her rip. It was quite a sight. The skiff didn't look fast, particularly with a rather rotund gentleman sitting in it. But given the right sea conditions, Dad could pass nearly everyone around.

The required condition is a slight chop, just enough to make it easy for the boat to break loose from the bonds of surface tension (which tends to cancel lift and keep a hull from planing) but not enough to cause the flat surface to pound. Pounding is the main drawback to a flat bottom and the reason you're more apt to see a planing table than a totally flat-bottomed planing boat larger than a skiff. Once the seas build up, a flat bottom will slam, pound, and otherwise bang into

Figure 3-1

BASIC PLANING PERFORMANCE   *Any flat surface will plane when it is trimmed properly. A proper planing hull, however, has more to it than a flat bottom.*

the water in a quite obnoxious manner. At first it is merely uncomfortable, but when the seas get high enough, the pounding counteracts forward motion sufficiently to take the boat off plane. So while they rate high on initial planing efficiency, flat bottoms rate low on total practicality.

Just the opposite might be said for the form known as the deep-V. Deep-Vs generally require more horsepower than other planing hulls but will continue to perform on plane and at speed under conditions that force other shapes to slow down. This is why offshore racers still often turn to the deep-V for rough water, as they have since Dick Bertram's *Moppie*, designed by C. Raymond Hunt, first showed her mettle by whipping everyone handily back in 1961. Also known as *constant deadrise* hulls because the deadrise doesn't change from bow to stern (Figure 3-2), the sharply angled bottom of a deep-V simply behaves toward the water beneath as the sharply angled bow of any boat does to the water ahead: cuts it like a knife. Since the cutting edge carries all the way aft, a deep-V can run with very little wetted surface (wetted surface equals friction, which equals reduced speed) and still cut into heavy seas by keeping only the extreme after portions of the hull in contact with the sea. Indeed, offshore racers often seem to have nothing but their drive units in the water.

Of course, deep-Vs are not perfect. In addition to needing more horsepower

Figure 3-2

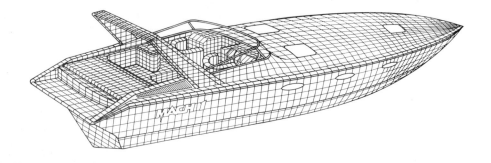

DEEP-V DEADRISE   *In this computer-generated model of a new Mach 1 Sovereign, note that the hull's 25-degree deadrise extends all the way to the transom—deep-Vs are also known as "constant deadrise" hulls. (Courtesy Mach 1)*

than other planing forms, they have a few other drawbacks. None is insurmountable, however, and many builders use deep-V hulls for boats that will be subjected to far less rigorous conditions than rough water offshore racing.

Deep-Vs have one particular performance habit that can be either blessing or curse, depending on circumstances: They run as straight as if they were on rails. When you *want* to go straight, it's wonderful. You can take a deep-V through surging following seas—the kind that tend constantly to push most other boats off course—or through a nasty inlet with ease. Hands off! The boat will hold itself true. But when you want to turn, it can be a different story. Then you often have a fight on your hands. A deep-V *will* turn, of course, but usually not as easily as other hull forms. If you have a deep-V, you definitely want power steering.

Given that a flat surface will plane more easily, it's not surprising that deep-Vs also have a tendency to lay over and run on one of the V's flats instead of on the apex. With every wave or so, the boat may flip from side to side in an action that undermines stability and makes control difficult. This action, logically called "chine walking," can be corrected to a large degree with modifications of the simple V form. Not so strangely, some of these modifications also alleviate other deep-V drawbacks as well.

Running strakes and chine flats (Figure 3-3) are the two principal additions. Running strakes are often considered to have cosmetic value only, but anyone who has ever suffered through the tribulations of conducting sea trials on a prototype deep-V (particularly back in the early days) will tell you that repositioning the strakes to their most effective location is a part of the drill. I will grant that their effect is minimal, but the small flats of the running strakes do *help* prevent chine walking. Chine flats help more. When the boat starts to heel, the lift provided by the flat surface at the extreme outboard edge will counter the heel and bring the boat back into proper trim. Chine flats also help deep-Vs with their

Figure 3-3

STRAKES AND FLATS   *The underbody shape of deep-V hulls usually includes running strakes and chine flats to increase lift and add lateral stability.*

lateral stability under low-speed or at-rest conditions. While the location of the center of gravity, beam, and other factors have influence also (as we saw with displacement hulls), the added lift at the extreme outboard edges helps considerably in keeping the boat upright in the displacement mode, though not as much as it does when the boat is moving fast. Indeed, deep-Vs are not often among the most stable boats at rest even with chine flats. However, many anglers use deep-V sportfishermen anyway, because they feel the boats' other attributes (particularly the ability to go fast in heavy seas) outweigh this minor drawback.

Another modification sometimes made to deep-V hulls is to flatten the extreme after end of the V—the part normally expected to be in contact with the water at all times. Usually called a "pad," this modification reflects the better planing efficiency of a flatter surface while allowing all the other attributes of a constant deadrise, since the hull still presents the cutting edge of the V forward of the pad. Pads are generally seen only on "performance" hulls.

Perhaps the ultimate departure is the so-called *modified-V.* Unlike the constant deadrise of a deep-V, the deadrise of a modified-V changes, starting out in the neighborhood of the deep-V at the bow (26 degrees or so) and flattening out to 18 to 14 degrees (or less) at the transom. For this reason, modified-Vs are also

Figure 3-4

MODIFIED-V *Also known as a "warped plane" hull, the modified-V starts with a sharp entry similar to a deep-V, but has a varying deadrise that flattens out to something on the order of 14 degrees at the transom.*

known as *variable deadrise* or *warped plane* hulls. The object is to retain cutting action forward and gain greater lift aft, which results in a more efficient hull that is easier to get on plane than a deep-V but less capable of handling the rough stuff at top speed. It is a practical compromise, so you will find that a lot of boats, from small open fishermen to fairly large motoryachts, do indeed sport warped plane bottoms. There are probably as many variations on the theme as there are builders and designers, and they all try to keep their designs proprietary. Differences are usually minor, however, and the truth is they often have better luck in getting a trademark for the *name* of the design than they do in claiming something exclusive, and therefore patentable, about the design itself.

One design which has been patented is the DeltaConic hull developed by Harry Schoell, an engineer and designer who lives and works in Fort Lauderdale, Florida. The DeltaConic hull is not, technically, a warped plane. The forward portions are of varying deadrise but take their form from sections of a cone. The after part is the delta, a $12^1/_2$-degree constant deadrise. The sections blend smoothly, and there are no compound curves involved (as there may be with some modified-V designs). The DeltaConic hull uses chine flats (actually angled slightly downward at the outboard edge) to provide some of its running stability, but relies on the fact that the delta sections and the conic sections have different rolling periods, which tend to cancel each other out, to gain stability when the hull is at rest. DeltaConic hulls are quite efficient and seakindly at just about any speed. Their major drawback, in my opinion, is that to work properly, all dimensions have to expand when the hull increases in length. Operationally, that's no problem; the form works at all sizes. But when you extend the length over 40 feet, the beam begins to exceed the width of many marinas' slips.

In Figure 3-5 we see a planing hull form quite common in smaller boats. Sometimes known as the *cathedral* hull, it is also (for obvious reasons) often called the *gull wing*. Its main attributes are performance similar to the deep-V and slightly better lateral stability—the outer wings give essentially the same aid to a planing hull as do the outriggers on a Polynesian dugout canoe.

Catamarans (Figure 3-6) work somewhat similarly but in effect eliminate the center portion and work on the "outriggers" alone. This gives the advantages of greater beam with less draft and less total wetted surface. That adds up to greater speed. Many of today's offshore races are won by catamarans, though as noted above they don't work as well in heavy seas, so racers frequently revert to the deep-V when the going gets rough. One possible exception to this is the cat developed by the late Don Aronow, a man who singlehandedly developed more

Figure 3-5

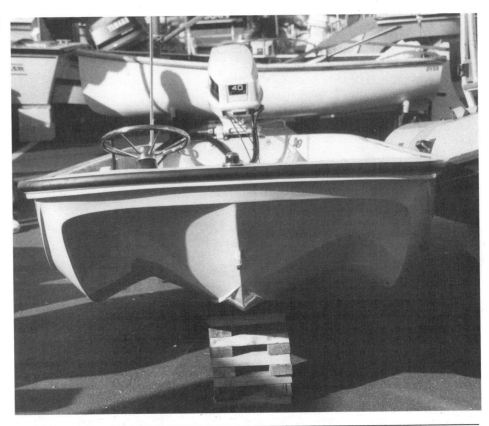

CATHEDRAL HULL   *This hullform offers considerable stability to narrow-beamed small boats by increasing buoyancy at the chines. It's easy to see why this design is also often called "gull-wing."*

Figure 3-6

CATAMARANS *Twin-hulled craft gain added lift and faster speeds as a result of the tunnel between the hulls. This version from Aronow Powerboats is essentially a deep-V that's been split in half and rejoined with the tunnel between. It seems to have the best virtues of both cats and deep-Vs. (Courtesy Aronow Powerboats)*

high-performance boats (and more high-performance boat companies) than any other individual. Slightly narrower than the traditional cat, the Aronow cat is simply a deep-V split in half and separated slightly. I say "simply" as if it were easy, yet deciding that this idea would work and determining exactly how wide the "split" should be were strokes of genius. The Aronow cats seem to thrive on heavy seas as much as traditional deep-Vs, but reportedly can go faster.

Planing Hull Performance

Since we choose a planing hull because we want to go faster, going faster often becomes the quest itself. If you recall our discussion in Chapter 1, you'll remember that speed on the water is a result of three factors: horsepower, weight, and shape. Since we are discussing planing hulls, we'll consider shape a constant for any particular boat and look at horsepower and weight as variables.

Horsepower

What happens when we up the power? Generally, we'll gain speed. But this isn't always the answer. Aside from limitations on the horsepower standard engines can deliver, there are other reasons why adding more power may not be the best alternative for increasing speed. As we have already seen, when you increase engine power, you usually increase engine weight (though there have been recent gains in this area, also, with new engines offering more horsepower per pound than was formerly available). And, of course, the added horsepower means burning more fuel, which means carrying more fuel (read: more weight— this hasn't changed) in order to have any kind of practical range. Sometimes the results are disappointing in that the added load cancels out the added horsepower for no net gain in performance. Even when it works, increasing horsepower may not be the answer. After all, you just might want your boat to be something more than engines and fuel tanks. So let's look for a better solution.

Weight

Planing results from hydrodynamic lift. And whether we're talking about a boat or a sack of groceries, the lighter the object, the easier it is to lift. So if we make the boat lighter, we'll get more lift and thus more speed from the same horses.

Yet, as logical as that statement seems, getting lighter boats has not been easy either. When we first started building with fiberglass, boats were usually heavier than they had to be. There were a number of reasons for this, ranging from seat-of-the-pants engineering, which tended to "add a little, just in case" to be sure the boat was strong enough, to consumers who wanted a plastic hull to thump as soundly and seem as thick as the wooden ones they had been used to. So most boats of quality were way overbuilt—which further bolstered consumer opinion that this is what a fiberglass boat should be. Because boatbuilders ultimately have to sell their product to the consumer, this belief made it difficult for engineers to sell better construction methods to the builders' marketing departments. And so it went. Though many current state-of-the-art techniques have been known since the mid 1970s, they were rarely used until a decade later except by racers and performance enthusiasts for whom the quest for speed overrides *everything*. As we enter the 1990s, many planing (and even some semidisplacement) hulls take full advantage of the latest weight-saving technology. I believe it won't be long before we can say "most" rather than "many."

Hull Construction

One of the most significant changes has been from solid FRP (fiberglass-reinforced plastic) construction to cored laminates. There's no question a lot of hull strength comes from hull thickness regardless of the material used—3/4-inch plywood can take a greater load than 1/2-inch. But there is no need for a plastic hull to be solid FRP. Look at an I beam. Its strength comes from the distance between the flanges. It will bear the same load as a solid piece of steel of like dimensions. The web need only be thick enough to keep the flanges apart under load. Similarly, a one-inch-thick hull will have the same strength whether it is solid FRP or has some other lighter material, or core, sandwiched between inner and outer FRP skins.

There are four generally used core materials: Baltek's end grain balsawood and three plastic foams—Airex, Divinycell, and Klegecell. Nomex, a paperlike honeycomb core material, has seen extensive use in sailboats but not so much as yet in the powerboat field. Naturally the makers of each product tout their own as being "best," but they are all good, each has strengths and weaknesses compared with the others (surprised?), and the main consideration is less which core

Figure 3-7

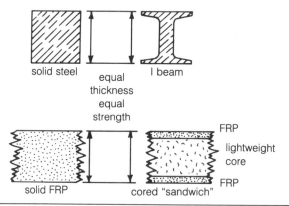

solid steel   equal   I beam
thickness
equal
strength

FRP
lightweight
core

solid FRP   cored "sandwich"   FRP

SANDWICH HULL CONSTRUCTION *Just as an I beam can possess the same strength as a similarly sized piece of solid steel, cored "sandwich" hulls can be as strong as a similar thickness of solid fiberglass-reinforced plastic (FRP).*

Figure 3-8

VACUUM BAGGING *This is one way of assuring a perfect core-to-skin bond. All the air is removed from the transparent vinyl bag so that atmospheric pressure will hold the balsa core tightly against the skin until the bonding resin is fully set up. (Forest Johnson photo courtesy Baltek and Bertram Yachts)*

is used than how well the core is bonded to the skins. The entire laminate—the inner and outer skins and the core—must remain a cohesive unit in order to have the desired strength. The technical and production difficulties involved in getting a good core-to-skin bond are also reasons many builders have been reluctant to change from solid to cored hulls despite their obvious advantage on a theoretical level. Solutions are available, however, and I think it is reasonable to conclude that conscientious builders will find ways to embrace them before releasing cored construction to the marketplace. That some still haven't changed to cored construction is, I believe, evidence of the validity of this conclusion. But the change is happening. Even those builders who are reluctant to use cored construction in high-stress areas, such as below the waterline, will often core topsides, superstructures, and interior bulkheads. And all builders seem willing to use some of the so-called exotics wherever feasible to improve their boats' strength-to-weight ratios.

A Closer Look at Fiberglass

In the beginning, the fiberglass in FRP boats came in three forms: cloth, which is the normal warp-and-weft woven material similar to any other kind of cloth but made of fiberglass strands rather than cotton, nylon, or other fiber; woven roving, which is simply a coarser weave; and chopped strand, which comprises random pieces of fiberglass filament. Because of its randomness and lack of any real interlocking connection between individual pieces of glass, chopped strand contributes the least strength to the laminate. It is often used as the outer layer, next to the gelcoat, to avoid *print-through,* the transfer of the woven fabric's texture to the surface. It is also a good filler, helping to maintain a good glass-to-resin ratio (too much of either reduces the laminate's strength) while building the total thickness faster than you can with cloth alone. It was, in its way, an early form of coring, a method of gaining thickness without added layers of cloth, though the weight saved is far less than with true core materials.

The need for chopped strand is lessened by using cored construction, but there will most likely always be some in every FRP boat. So please let me burst another balloon.

Chopped strand gets into a laminate by either of two methods. In the hand layup method, the strands are first lightly bound into sheets of mat which can be handled much like cloth. The binder merely holds the strands together in workable form until the layers of mat (and cloth or roving) can be wetted out by application of resin and hand rolling. The other method is called *chopper gun* because the "gun" which sprays on the resin also cuts or chops continuous filaments of glass into strands that get blown into the laminate along with the resin.

Hand layup proponents often try to sell that method as best and imply that chopper gun construction is a shoddy substitute. The truth is that once they are included in a good laminate with a proper balance of resin to glass (usually 65/35), the chopped strands don't care how they got there. And neither should you. It is good to know which method was used on a boat you are considering, because it helps in following up on the builder's quality control. When either method is handled properly, the result is the same: a good laminate. However, the opportunities for fouling up are different and unique to each. Hence, each requires its own type of quality control.

With hand layup, the main problem is improper wet-out—i.e., not getting a thorough penetration of resin. This leads to resin-poor sections that may delaminate easily under stress. This can usually be detected during layup, and conscientious builders watch each mold carefully to avoid the problem.

Chopper guns are faster and, when properly adjusted, eliminate inadequate wet-out. But a maladjustment can lead to either too little or too much glass for the amount of resin applied. This cannot be as easily judged during application, because the result will look much the same no matter what. Good chopper gun builders will lab test the plugs cut out of the hulls for such purposes as cooling water intakes or ports. By weighing the plugs before and after baking them in a high-temperature oven, they can easily determine the glass-to-resin ratio, because the resin burns out in baking. The best builders check plugs frequently enough to correct chopper gun adjustment before the resulting laminates get beyond tolerance. That means every hull will be within acceptable standards.

In addition to basic cloth, woven roving, and chopped strand, we now have nonwoven biaxials, triaxials, and a multitude of unidirectional fabrics, which have their greatest strength in specific directions. We also have CoreMat, Fabmat, and various other materials that were unknown only a few years ago. By taking advantage of each material's particular attributes, engineers can now design laminates that gain their strength by use of the *right* material rather than by using *more* material. This too has contributed to great gains in the strength-to-weight department.

In some cases, we've actually gotten away from using fiberglass in "fiberglass" boats and use Kevlar for the reinforcing fabric (KRP?), while other boats use a Kevlar/fiberglass mixture. If you consider that Kevlar is also the material of flak jackets and bulletproof vests, you'll understand how it can add strength without weight by reducing the need for more layers of a weaker fabric. Kevlar's main drawback is that it costs more than glass; since it takes special tools and techniques to cut the stuff and it can be used in a "drier" laminate (which requires more careful handwork), the layup labor costs are higher, too.

Carbon fiber rods, with a tensile strength five times greater than steel, are often used to reinforce high-stress areas such as stringers, chines, and gunwales, providing considerably more strength with little added weight.

We've also seen changes in resin. Epoxy has long been known to be stronger than the traditional polyester resin but has often been bypassed because of its greater cost. In recent years we've seen the wider use of such new materials as vinylester resin, which wets out more easily (especially with some of the more exotic fabrics) and remains more flexible than polyester. When used with Kevlar, for example, vinylester permits a 50/50 resin-to-fabric ratio rather than the 65/35 ratio generally used in standard glass construction. Vinylester resin is also more resistant to water absorption than polyester, which makes it a natural for boat construction by eliminating the problem of blistering. But it, too, costs more.

Of course *all* weight-saving technology generally costs more than plain old solid FRP. Which means a light boat will probably be a more expensive boat—to buy. Since it will gain the same performance from lower horsepower, it should burn less fuel, which means it will inevitably be a less expensive boat to run. If you use your boat a lot, the higher initial cost could add up to a lower total cost.

Trim and Stability

The one thing that can be said about all planing hulls is that they are sensitive to trim. The table in Figure 3-1 and my dad's tubby skiff were able to plane only because of the way they were trimmed. But all planing hulls deliver better performance when they are trimmed correctly—you can see an increase in speed and engine rpm without touching the throttles when you reach optimum trim. In fact, the "throttleman" in an offshore racer is actually controlling trim as much as engine speed to keep the boat at its highest performance level.

The reason is simple: The hydrodynamic lift which results in planing is due, to a large degree, to the angle at which the hull meets the water. Change the angle and you change performance.

Well-balanced planing hulls seem to rise on plane and settle back down with little change in running angle. Others need to climb out of the "hole" before they attain a planing attitude, and tend to squat again when you back off on the throttles. This is not necessarily bad. In fact, it often can't be helped. Aft-cabin cruisers and small boats in which engine weight is a disproportionate amount of the total weight are prime examples; the only way they could be balanced would be to carry unnecessary weight forward, which would be detrimental to total performance.

It is, however, wise to equip such hulls with trimmable drive systems such as outboards or sterndrives when possible—conventional underwater running gear just doesn't work as well. It's also reason to use adjustable electro-hydraulic trim tabs no matter what kind of drive system you have. Some boats can perform

Figure 3-9

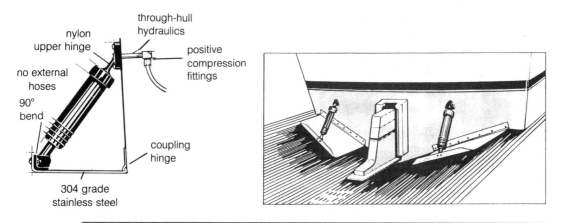

KEEPING TABS ON LIFT *Adjustable trim tabs are an excellent means of adding stern lift and lateral trim to planing hulls. Just be sure to have them all the way up when running inlets or in following seas—two of the few times you absolutely do not want added stern lift. (Courtesy Bennett Marine)*

adequately without such aids, and their designers often adamantly resist adding them. But this is true only when the boat is properly balanced—a condition not always easy to attain under real world conditions. Tabs give you the option of maintaining trim underway even if other factors are working to disrupt the delicate balance. They are particularly valuable in keeping a deep-V upright when it wants to lean a bit. In short, there are very few planing hulls that won't benefit from some trim tab action at some time or other, even if that action isn't needed all the time. That's why I'm pleased to report that while some builders still offer trim tabs as optional accessories, most now recognize the wisdom of having them available even if you don't always need them, and include tabs as standard equipment.

Planing hull stability is similar to displacement hull stability except that in the planing mode we have other forces at work. The hydrodynamic lift that makes the hull plane also tends, to a large degree, to offset external forces that might lead to rolling. That's the good news. The bad news is that the lift is only there at planing speeds. Slow down, and there goes your stability. Worse news: In our quest for lightness to provide higher speeds with less horsepower, we may develop boats that are so light they bob like a cork unless they are moving fast. The worst news: Antiroll devices, which will help displacement and even semidisplacement hulls, tend to get in the way on fast-moving planing hulls. So we are left with different approaches to low-speed stability in fast-moving boats.

A very common one is to forget the problem and develop a boat that just goes fast! Nice work if you can get it, but you often can't. Which means being very uncomfortable when you can't throttle up. Other builders and designers try to take a more pragmatic approach and work out a hull form with a degree of at-rest and low-speed stability built in. Some succeed better than others, but on the whole we have to face the truth that fast boats usually ride better going fast. When you sea trial a planing boat, don't get carried away with seeing how fast it will go and how quickly it gets on plane. These points are important, of course, but be sure to include some slow running and a stop or two to see if you can live with the boat under those conditions as well. While no boat will ever be 100 percent comfortable 100 percent of the time, you want one that approaches this goal as closely as possible, or you won't be happy with it. Remember, comfort is a subjective thing, and in stability as with other aspects, you and your family must be the final judges of what is comfortable for you.

Now that we've seen the advantages and disadvantages of slow boats and fast boats, let's turn our attention to those that fall somewhere between.

———————◆———————

4. Semidisplacement Hulls

The first thing to say about semidisplacement hulls is that some people claim there is no such animal. This school of thought maintains that a hull either planes or it doesn't. Simple as that. I think these people also see the world in black and white. Not only do they miss the colors, they don't even recognize gray!

Another group maintains that semidisplacement boats are really displacement boats that manage to trick Mother Nature into believing they have a longer waterline. This, of course, creates a speed-to-length ratio higher than 2.0, though the boat is still in the displacement mode (Figure 4-1).

And yet another group maintains that these boats should be called *semiplaning* rather than semidisplacement, because they "sort of" plane, though not to the degree we observe in pure planing hulls.

To me, the determining (and defining) element is bow action. If the forefoot remains in the water, it's a displacement hull. If it gets clear, and the bow wave begins abaft the forefoot, the hull is planing. If it's *almost* clear, the hull is semidisplacement. To give the either/or crowd their due, perhaps a semidisplacement

A SEMIDISPLACEMENT HULL   *Observe that the bow wave doesn't crest again until it is well behind the transom, yet the forefoot is indeed still in the water, a clear indication that the boat is moving through the water rather than over it.*

hull is actually an underpowered (or overweight) planing hull. I would buy that except that semidisplacement hulls seem to run better in the displacement mode than do most pure planing hulls. Perhaps that is part of the answer, too, in that the underwater lines which contribute to better displacement performance may somehow detract from pure planing performance. Maybe it's all academic and best reserved for those endless, never resolved discussions we boatmen often have over a cool one or two at a dockside bar. The bottom line is that if the boat exceeds pure displacement hull speed yet doesn't show a speed-to-length ratio greater than 4.0, it must be, by definition, *semidisplacement*. And since we are looking for the pluses and minuses inherent in every possibility, it is really only these aspects of performance that concern us. So let's not bother with the whys and hows; let's just look at the whats.

Many years ago, Johnny Mercer wrote a song called *Accentuate the Positive* in which he cautioned us to "eliminate the negative and don't mess with Mister

Figure 4-2

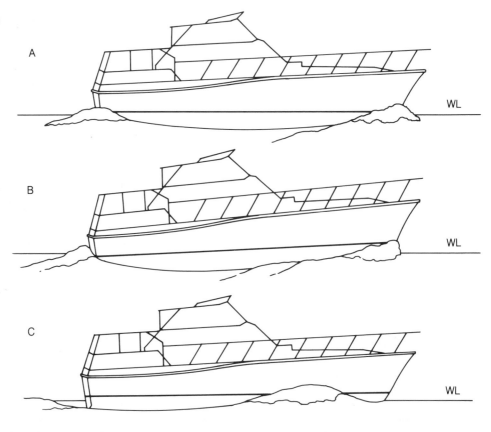

CLIMBING OUT OF THE HOLE *A semidisplacement boat will often exhibit relatively inefficient performance as it moves out of the pure displacement mode (A). The stern digs in, the bow wave gets deeper but not longer, and you simply burn more fuel and make more noise as you try to climb out of the "hole" (B), until you can lift the boat over the "hump" and begin to semiplane (C).*

In-between." When it comes to semidisplacement hulls, the positive is that they *are* in-between. Not as slow as pure displacement hulls, they can still carry more of a payload than a pure planing hull. Whether this is the best or the least of both worlds depends on your objectives. For many, the ability to have a decent cabin, room for the whole family, enough stowage for a practical cruise (two weeks, for example), and still not be limited to displacement speeds is all the argument they need. To others, the "semi" prefix means the boat is either not fast enough or doesn't have enough load capacity to suit them.

The semidisplacement compromise makes sense for a lot of applications, and that's the reason many large family cruisers and motoryachts have this type of hull. It isn't perfect, and it can't be all things to all people, but it *is* a very reasonable general-purpose hull, delivering acceptable performance at displacement speeds and faster.

One thing you'll notice about many semis is that they are much like pure displacement hulls and stern-heavy planing hulls through a certain portion of the power curve. Throttle up to maximum displacement speed, and from then until you have enough power to get out of the hole and over the "hump" you only burn more fuel and make more noise. Once you apply enough power, the stern lifts and the semiplaning activity begins. Needless to say, running the boat at any throttle setting between "max displacement" and "over the hump" is just wasting fuel. It also should be obvious that trim tabs can help here, too, making the stern lift a little more easily and quickly.

5•Comparing the Three Hull Types

Now that we've had an opportunity to look at the three major hull forms, it's time to go further and look at some of their similarities and differences.

One of the big factors affecting hull performance is at-rest draft. Displacement hulls will sit deep in the water because they can and should. As we saw in Chapter 2, this gives them their load-carrying abilities and a big part of their low-speed stability. Planing hulls, on the other hand, should be shallow draft (relatively speaking) so that there is less distance to go in lifting the hull up onto the surface to plane. As you'd expect, semis fall in between and never do quite get up onto a full plane even at wide-open throttle (though they generally leave pure displacement performance far behind). Since they leave more boat in the water than pure planing hulls, semidisplacement boats can usually benefit from stabilizers as much as displacement hulls do. Unfortunately, many builders seem reluctant to include them as standard equipment. A colleague of mine, Charles Nichols, and I have been on a soapbox of late trying to get them more generally accepted by builders. Given the draft limitations placed on all pleasure craft (and especially those we want to move faster than displacement speeds) coupled with our desire for all sorts of creature comforts, which can only add weight aloft, it is not an admission of "poor design" to include an antiroll device any more than it is to include trim tabs. Both systems add to the enjoyment of boating, and in my opinion it is wrong to make the consumer have to choose them as extras. They belong aboard and should be included in the initial construction and in the base price. I believe it's best for all concerned.

Locating the waterline is one of the many calculations that naval architects must make in designing a hull. To do this, they use a figure termed "pounds-per-inch immersion." This figure, which is simply the weight it takes to set the boat an inch lower into the water, is directly related to its cross-sectional area at the waterline. (Cross-sectional area at the waterline is also known as *waterline plane* — remember this term because we'll see it again shortly.) While pounds-per-inch immersion is primarily a concern of the designer and builder, it can also be important to the operator in that it helps you determine how much gear and provisions you can bring aboard without adversely affecting performance and stability.

In Figure 5-1 we see athwartship cross-sectional views of three boats that have similarities above the waterline. Beam, freeboard, and overall length are nearly identical. Boat A is simply more boat! Remember that it takes more weight to sit deeper in the water. Boat A will inevitably have a greater fuel and potable water capacity, heavier construction, and probably more living space and creature comforts aboard, or it wouldn't sit as deep. On the other hand, boats B and C *can't* have as much aboard or they couldn't sit as high. If we were to load either B or C to the point where they would weigh the same as boat A, we would reduce freeboard to a dangerous point in B and to a critical point in C (there would be so little freeboard the slightest wave could flood it). A is a displacement hull, B semidisplacement, and C planing. It should be no surprise that boat A will have the greatest initial stability, and boat C will have the highest speed.

Now let's see what I mean by "more boat." In Figure 5-2 we see profile views of the boats we've just discussed. Boat A sits deep enough in the water to carry considerable weight aloft. She can have an open upper deck, or bridge deck, that includes a spacious flying bridge with lots of usable guest seating at its forward

Figure 5-1

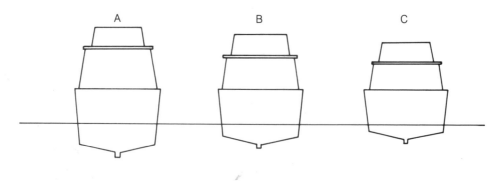

DISPLACEMENT AND DRAFT   *While all three hulls show similar freeboard and beam at their midsections, their underbodies reveal three quite different boats. Boat A is a displacement hull, boat B, semidisplacement, and boat C, planing.*

end, and probably a wet bar, a fair-sized dinghy, and maybe even a motor scooter and Jet-Ski or two.

Boat A can carry this load aloft because of the weight she carries below. With this hull depth there can be a full-length standing-headroom lower deck. This in

Figure 5-2

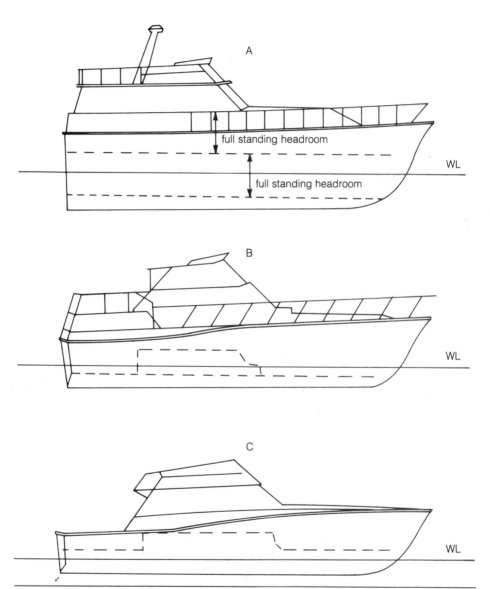

PROFILES OF PERFORMANCE *These are the same boats we saw in Figure 5-1. All are about 55 feet long overall, 50 feet on the waterline. Boat A, the displacement hull, permits the most variety in accommodation plans. Two full-length decks, both with full standing headroom, grant considerable flexibility. Even the engine room can be located anywhere from fully astern to amidships. Boats B and C offer less flexibility and less room for accommodations but will inevitably be faster.*

turn means walk-in engine room(s), and if the overall length is in the 50-foot-plus-range, probably three staterooms plus crew quarters with private heads for each.

The main deck can house a saloon, dining area, galley, wet bar and, if desired, an inside console—again all on one continuous deck. Because of the hull depth and weight required to attain the design draft, fuel and water capacity will be substantially greater than in boats B and C.

Boat B will have to be what we would call a "split level" if we were discussing houses. There isn't room for a continuous deck at any level. There would likely be a raised aft deck to allow headroom in the stateroom (or two) beneath it. From there you could go up to a flying bridge or down to the saloon. The walk-around portion of the foredeck would probably be at a different level from either the aft deck or the saloon sole.

The bridge would have to be smaller than on boat A simply because this boat can't carry as much weight that high. With the bridge above the saloon, head-room requirements in the saloon would push the saloon sole low enough to re-duce the engine compartment beneath it to a crawl space.

Traditionally styled hulls are deeper forward, so we would probably find a galley and dinette down and forward from the saloon, and another stateroom in the bow.

This arrangement is practical, and you'll find it (or a variation of the theme) in many motoryachts from 35 to 60 feet. It is a fine compromise but doesn't offer the total comfort or space we saw in the similarly sized displacement boat A.

Boat C will have to have a lot less in the way of living space to keep total weight down. In this case we are probably looking at a "convertible," which will have a saloon with galley up and two staterooms and a single shared head down and forward. I have drawn it with little weight aloft— mostly in a small but functional flying bridge. If you were to use it as a sportfisherman, it could probably stand to carry an aluminum tuna tower as long as other weight is kept low in the boat.

The greater hull depth of boat A offers a couple of other advantages I should also mention. Because the lower deck and main deck are both full length and full height, you are less restricted in the placement of bulkheads and other interior design features. The accommodations plans of both B and C are somewhat dictated by the "split-levels" inherent in the designs. Perhaps more important, boat A can have watertight bulkheads below deck because every bulkhead can be a *full* bulkhead, vertically as well as horizontally. The arrangements of B and C require more openness and often allow only partial bulkheads, since there is no "lower deck" per se. The locations of stairways are also dictated by the require-ments of the levels, and they, too, often preclude dividing the hull into watertight compartments. Boats B and C could have watertight engine compartments but probably no further subdivision.

As I said, the waterline and stability of the boat as built are the designer and builder's responsibilities; after that it's up to you. Unfortunately, some skippers ignore these factors, and the sad truth is that overloading and improper loading are among the leading causes of small-boat mishaps.

Say you have a 26-foot center-console fisherman and decide to add a tower for better visibility. You can, provided you don't go too high. But once you have the tower, it doesn't mean you can invite all your fishing buddies to come up there with you! Whatever you do with any boat, you have to keep the weight relatively low to keep the center of gravity low. You might wonder who would be so foolish as to let everybody ride on the tower of a small boat, but should you ignore the advice to keep weight low, you would not be the first to do so.

And what about overloading? Well, it is perhaps more of a small-boat problem, related to those who would rather ignore their dinghy's capacity plate than make an extra trip. But overloading bigger boats can have its drawbacks, too, even if the potential for danger is less. A few years ago I was involved in the management of a 58-foot motoryacht with a semidisplacement hull. It had belonged to the same owner for ten years. When we had the bottom redone to eliminate the "dead" antifouling paint that had built up over the decade and remove the blisters that had formed, we decided we should raise the waterline a couple of inches to effect a better exposure of antifouling action—the original waterline had been underwater for some time. About a year after that, the owner sold the boat and unloaded eleven years' worth of accumulated personal belongings. When I delivered the boat to its new owner, the painted waterline was 3 inches above the water and the boat cruised 2 knots faster than it did before the owner removed his gear!

Bottoms, Topsides, and Fine Points of Form

One factor affecting performance in all hull types is the cleanliness of the bottom. Bottom paint is usually an option, and the choice of brands is left to the buyer and dealer. There's a good reason for this: The bottom paint you should use depends not only on what sort of boat you have (fast boats need a slicker finish), but also on where you do your boating. If you operate your boat on fresh water or store it on a trailer, you won't need bottom paint at all. The builder can't possibly put the same paint on every boat, which means applying the paint is often left to the dealer (though many builders will apply the paint of your choice—as an option—before initial launching). A word of advice: Antifouling paint is probably the most expensive paint you'll ever buy. Even the least costly options are dear. But this is not the place to cut corners. If you love your boat, use the best paint you can. For your particular boat and boating area, it may turn out that you don't need the most expensive paint available, but heed your dealer's advice. I repeat: Use the best paint you can get. It will pay in the long run in better performance and lower operating cost. Then too, many paints that cost more initially do deliver better performance for a longer time, and thus cost less in the hauling and painting department.

There are a few features you should consider in every hull type except the deep-V, which is a different bird and can get away with breaking the rules. Some of these features may be seen in deep-Vs, and if so, OK. For the most part they won't do any harm. But the benefits they give to other hulls just aren't generally needed by deep-Vs.

Fine Entry

The sharper the knife, the swifter the cut. The same holds true for the bows of boats. A fine, sharp entry cuts the water better and allows the boat to slice

Figure 5-3

FINE ENTRY *A sharp angle at the forefoot, as we see in this Symbol 44 MKII, almost guarantees a smooth ride by cutting the seas like a knife. (Courtesy Symbol Yachts)*

through oncoming waves rather than pound into them. The result in a displacement mode is a steadier, smoother forward progression, and the same is true in semidisplacement boats. In planing boats, the fine entry should carry back abaft the forefoot, because this area, too, will be cutting the water when the boat gets on plane.

A very fine entry can make for a wet boat because the water cut by the bow will fly upward rather than out (a blunt bow pushes the water away rather than up). There are remedies for this, however. One of the simplest is to install spray rails just above the waterline. They will knock the water back down and away from the boat before the wind can catch it and bring it aboard as spray.

Flare

A bow with a lot of flare will also tend to keep spray in its place. More important, however, is the reserve buoyancy it provides. Buoyancy is influenced by shape in that pounds-per-inch immersion is directly related to the area of waterline plane. If the hull angles out rapidly (flares), the waterline plane expands rapidly with increasing height above the design waterline, and the deeper the hull is immersed the more it resists still deeper immersion. This is particularly important forward, though a slight outward angle is good all along the topsides. A

Figure 5-4

FLARE   *The shadow under the gunwales at the bow of this Jersey 42 sportfisherman is a result of flare. This shape (traditional along the Jersey shore) assures more than adequate reserve buoyancy and, usually, a dry ride. (Courtesy Jersey Yachts)*

flaring bow tends to keep the bow in an "up" attitude, which is good for longitudinal stability and for a smoother ride. Deep-Vs do not need flare, because at high speed they are wont to run on surfaces so far abaft the bow it doesn't matter. And since a deep-V bow tends to lift anyway, flare can actually be detrimental to control by providing too much wind lift. That's one good reason racing hulls and their derivatives usually have a reverse-sheer "needle-nosed" bow.

Freeboard

That's the term for the distance from the waterline to the gunwales. The more the better, generally speaking, because it gives you room to play with in loading and trimming your boat. As we saw earlier, overloading causes a boat to sink below its design waterline. Whether this is merely a detriment to optimum performance or a serious threat to safety depends, to a great degree, on how much freeboard remains. The more freeboard you start with, the more reserve you have.

Beam

In Chapter 2 we saw how greater beam helps increase stability in displacement hulls. It does the same for semidisplacement and planing hulls. Further, because spreading a similar weight over a greater area increases buoyancy (it's that waterline plane again), a wider beamed boat can actually plane more easily because it will likely have a shallower draft to begin with. Again, the exception is the deep-V, which usually works better in narrower hulls. The deep-V's beam is partly dictated by the points at which the bottom of a 26-degree deadrise hull will cut the plane formed by the topsides, although a designer can gain a little beam by working with the chine flats. Some deep-Vs employ a double chine, bringing one set of flats into play at rest and at displacement speeds, while the second "kicks in" at speed. This allows a deep-V to be wider than the basic lines might indicate.

By the way, beamier boats offer another advantage, too. They give you more boat for the money in marinas and boatyards. Most facilities charge by the foot—of length overall. A 27-foot boat with a 10-foot beam permits you more amenities than a 27-footer with an 8-foot beam, but either boat will incur the same fees at most marinas and yards.

Higher Math and Other Nonsense

There are formulas you can use to determine a lot of things about a boat's performance simply by considering its dimensions against other factors such as displacement weight or volume. The result is generally a coefficient which, when applied to another of the figures involved, will give you a performance indicator. But you really don't have to know about waterplane coefficient, prismatic coefficient, block coefficient, or any other such esoteric factor to determine the right boat for you. For one thing, most salespeople would be totally inept to answer a question regarding any of the above, and I dare say that after as brief an explanation as I'd have room for here, you would be as hard-pressed to understand the answer if it could be given. Naval architects and engineers must work with these factors to develop a boat that will do what we want, but for our purposes, all we need to see is what it will do on the water. To hell with theory! If it rides the way we like and has the speed and other features we want, it's right. If it doesn't, it isn't. Keep looking. It's as simple as that.

Of course, when we find a boat we like, it is nice to be able to judge whether it is suitable in *every* way. That is, how can we be sure the boat of our dreams has the level of quality we want before we make such a major investment? There are ways. And Charles Nichols once summed them up quite nicely in a "Ship's Systems" column in *Power and Motoryacht* magazine. Since I can't think of a better way to put it myself, with his kind permission I include them here.

Ten Clues to Quality

In each of the following ten checkpoints, what you are really looking for is *care*—in one of several phases of the construction process.

1. The first place to check is the finish itself. Here, we are looking for care in the development of the tooling—the plug and mold from which the hull is made—and care in this particular boat's layup. Study the hull surface obliquely, and you can tell a lot. We used to look for print-through, the pattern of the woven roving or cloth showing through the gelcoat. The better the hull, the less you'd see. Since most builders now use a layer of mat or another patternless material immediately beneath the gelcoat, this problem has been essentially eliminated, but there are still things you can spot.

Fortunately, shiny surfaces aren't forgiving of imperfections that lie beneath. When you look down along the hull surface you'll see something ranging from absolute perfection—a totally smooth, flawless shine no matter what the angle of view—to disaster, where you can spot the location of every interior bulkhead by its telltale bulge, and "flat" places are anything but. Most production boats will lie somewhere between. Look closely at reflections of straight lines (fluorescent tubes overhead can be a big help). The better the hull, the straighter and sharper they'll be. A little waviness is acceptable, but shy away from a hull that shows too much.

2. Next, look at the electrical system. True, most of it is hidden. But what you can see—if you look closely—speaks volumes about the system (and the boat) as a whole.

Check out the distribution panels. Look for an ample number of circuits (including blank spares). When several items must share the same fuse or breaker, trouble in one means the potential loss of all. And give points for using breakers only. Fuses are OK, of course, but they add the drawback of having to stock spares and the possibility of your fouling things up further by replacing a blown fuse with one of the wrong amperage.

Look for ample metering on the panels. Voltmeters for both AC and DC are the minimum. Ammeters help you avoid overload. If you have a genset, a frequency meter is almost a must. With 120-volt AC dockpower, a reverse-polarity indicator is also essential.

If you can, take a peek behind the panel. Color-coded wiring and markers at each terminal are good signs.

3. Plumbing systems are also good quality checks, though there are fewer places to look. Among the signs of better quality: seacocks or ball valves rather than gate valves on through-hulls, double clamps on critical hose connections (all those beneath the waterline and anywhere else a broken connection would be more than an inconvenience), and reinforced hose on suction lines.

Figure 5-5

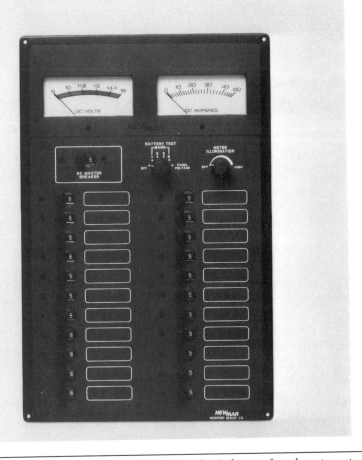

A PROPER ELECTRICAL PANEL *One good sign of overall quality is the use of good components. For example, a good electrical panel will feature ample circuits (including spares), circuit breakers rather than fuses, and metering for both voltage and current. (Courtesy Newmar)*

4. Look again at the electrical and plumbing systems as a whole, with an eye for neatness. The neater the workmanship, the better the boat. Look for straight runs with definite turns at each change of direction and solid support along the way. Better wiring will be bundled, or run in chases or flexible conduit.

A neat installation suggests good materials. It's no guarantee, but because the greater cost will be in the labor, a builder will rarely pay someone to do a proper job of installing inferior stuff.

Look for labels on switches, valves, junction boxes, pipes, and wires. The more the better, because they can tell you more than just what's written on them. Not only will they make it easier to learn your way around your new boat, they also show the builder's care in helping you do so.

5. See how things fit. Back when boats were all wood inside and out, interior joinerwork was an indicator of unseen workmanship. It still is to a degree, in that good woodwork reflects overall care of building. Even in a boat that substitutes molded interior components for joinery, you can get a hint of the level of engineering and quality control involved by studying how the modular units fit together. Sloppy fits, if present, will be readily apparent. The better things are where you can see, the better the chances of their being fine where you can't.

6. Check for watertight integrity. In hull lengths up to 25 feet or so, one compartment is OK, but unless you have an open outboard-powered runabout, a bigger boat should have at least two independent, watertight compartments. I'm pleased to report that many builders today are isolating the engine compartment and making all the through-hull penetrations there. This lessens the chances of water intrusion into the cabin area.

Needless to say, there should be at least one bilge pump for each watertight compartment. Ideally, there will be a manual backup for the engine compartment and some means of extending its suction to other areas.

7. Ask about the hardware. It all shines when new. But chrome-plated Zamak (a zinc alloy) will not stand up to salt nearly as well as chrome-plated bronze or stainless steel. Many builders are opting for the lesser shine of Marinium hardware. This anodized aluminum alloy isn't quite as tough as stainless but seems to stand up nearly as well.

In handrails, welded one-piece units are better than separate sections held together by yet more pieces of connecting hardware. Welded rails are more solid to begin with and will stay that way.

Look for ample cleats, chocks, and fairleads, and make sure that there are no sharp or rough edges that can damage your lines.

8. Look into the way the hardware is attached. Fiberglass doesn't hold screws well. It's better if hardware is through-bolted using a backing plate of hardwood, stainless steel, or aluminum. Hardwood backing plates are comparatively bulky and require large washers on the bolts; aluminum plates are good if well constructed; stainless steel is probably the best alternative other than bronze, which is rarely seen anymore. Another good method replaces the core of a deck sandwich locally with aluminum, the hardware being then held by machine

Figure 5-6

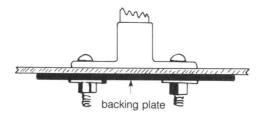

backing plate

THE BETTER BACK-UP *Fiberglass doesn't hold screws very well. Be sure that handrail stanchions and other load-bearing elements are through-bolted with adequate backing plates. (Courtesy* Power and MotorYacht *Magazine)*

screws threaded into the aluminum. Not so good is a hardwood backing plate with wood screws to hold the hardware, though it is slightly better than screws into plain fiberglass.

9. Look for built-ins (electronics, galley appliances, etc.). Many boats today are offered as a complete package. For those that aren't, there should still be ample room to add the extras, preferably as built-ins. This means blank spaces on or around the console, and easy access to run the wiring they'll need.

10. Ask to see a hull cutout plug. Few hull penetrations are molded in; they are cut. This means there is a piece of scrap (or plug) for each hole. Many builders destroy one plug in quality control, but some plugs should still be available, especially when yet more hull penetrations are made by the dealer. Lack of available plugs for inspection does not mean poor quality, but obviously the more pride the builder and dealer have in the quality of layup, the more likely they are to be anxious to show you a piece of cross section.

If you recall the adage about free lunches, you'll realize that each of these quality indicators has its price. The better the boat, the more you'll probably have to pay. But using them can be a big help in understanding why two outwardly similar boats can have such different price tags. Quality costs initially, but it pays in the long run.

———————◆———————

6•Drive Systems

Just when you think you have all the options under control, you get hit with the question, "What kind of power?" Gas, diesel, single screw, twin screw, conventional drive, V-drive, sterndrive, inboard, outboard, surface piercing, jet ... Whew! Your choice of power train involves perhaps more options than type and style of boat. Again, each offers advantages and, of course, concomitant drawbacks. Just as you can work through the maze of boats to find the one best for you, you can do it with power systems, too.

Since we have to start somewhere, let's begin with the conventional inboard drive system—engine(s) inside the boat and shaft(s), prop(s), and rudder(s) beneath it. There's historical precedent for this, because in the early days of powerboats, it was the only choice.

In conventional drives these days, our choices generally come down to gasoline or diesel, and single or twin screw. We'll also try to put the drive system itself into perspective, so you can see how conventional underwater running gear stacks up against other choices.

Gas or Diesel?

Gas engines cost less. All inboard engines adapted for marine use are derived from standard car, truck, or industrial engines. Because there are more gasoline-burning cars than other vehicles on the road, engines designed for this application are more plentiful and thus less expensive to begin with—greater volume of production equals lower cost per unit. True, the cost of marinization is similar for all engines and depends more on size than type, but when the block and those other components which are identical whether the engine will be used on the road or off cost less, the final product has to cost less also.

Gasoline engines are lighter. Great strides have been made in this department, and some new diesels offer astounding horsepower-to-weight ratios. But on the whole, if you are trying to keep the weight of the boat down, gas engines will help.

Gas engine *parts* are often more readily available and less expensive. Because the engines themselves are more common on both highways and waterways, their parts tend to be around in greater abundance also. Please note, however, that in most cases, though automotive equivalents will usually fit marinized engines, safety dictates using certified marine components because automobiles don't require the "ignition protection" under the hood that is mandatory in marine engine compartments.

This brings us to gasoline's biggest drawback. Its ability to explode easily (which makes it such a good fuel inside the engine) makes it potentially dangerous to have aboard. I say potentially, because while gasoline can be very dangerous indeed, it doesn't have to be. Gasoline does require a greater degree of care

Figure 6-1

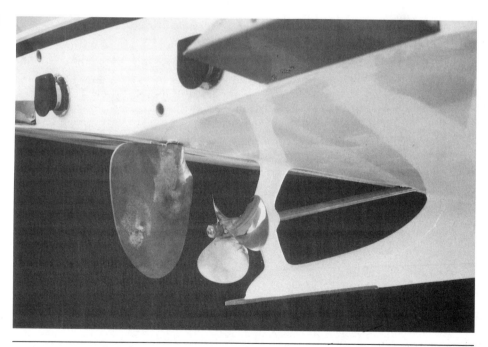

PROPULSION AND STEERING *The propeller provides the push, the rudder gives direction. Note the shaft angle, and the under-propeller protection that is possible when you use a single screw. (Keel Drive photo courtesy Shamrock Marine)*

in handling and certain precautions in all areas—care and precautions that quite simply can be forgotten if you use diesel oil for fuel. However, a properly built boat (as are those on the market today) that is properly maintained and operated (and that's up to you) will be safe no matter what its fuel.

Realistically, this means that while using diesel allows you to let your guard down in some areas, you can't be totally complacent. Diesel won't explode like gasoline, but even diesel fuel calls for certain maintenance and operational procedures to keep your boat fire-safe; gasoline just calls for a few more.

The big thing you have to keep in mind is that hydrocarbon vapors are heavier than air. In a car this is no problem; any gasoline vapor present outside the engine sinks—to the ground, where it dissipates in the open air. In a boat, what goes down collects in the bilges, and unless you take precautions to keep the bilges scoured with plenty of fresh air, the collected vapors can reach the lower explosive limit (LEL) and go "boom." Experienced boatmen are well aware of this and make keeping their bilges clean—*in every way*—a number-one priority.

Though they cost more initially, diesels can cost less in the long run. The drastic differences in fuel prices of 20 years ago, when diesel was only about half the cost of gas, are unlikely to return, but diesel is still usually at least a few cents less per gallon than gas. Diesel engines also usually turn out more usable power (torque) per gallon, so the fuel stretches a little further. But the big difference shows up if you put a lot of hours on your boat. Diesel engines last longer than gas engines. They usually come from the truck and industrial world and are built tougher (which is another reason they cost more initially). This means you can run diesel engines harder and longer before you have to consider major overhaul or replacement.

Not too many years ago I would have had to say that diesel engines are not only generally heavier, they are physically bigger, too. This is no longer universally true. There are now a number of diesels on the market that will fit the same space (and often the same mounts) as the more popular large gas engines.

When you get into maxi-engines for megayachts, the field is almost exclusively diesel, but for boats up to about 50 feet long, the bottom line is probably whether you would rather pay more initially but less in the long run (diesel) or have a lower purchase price but potentially greater operating and maintenance cost (gas). Some boats come only one way or the other, but with the proliferation of smaller, lighter diesels you will undoubtedly be faced with an even greater variety of choices in the future.

Single or Twins?

If single-screw boats didn't work, a majority of the world's commercial fishing fleets would never leave port. For many boats in most situations, a single screw is fine. Granted, single-screw boats are not quite as maneuverable, but speaking as one who spent a number of years operating large, single-screw commercial vessels, I can honestly say that in the hands of an experienced skipper, a single-screw boat can do almost anything a twin-screw boat can do. However, that "almost" is important. We'll get into boathandling later in the book; for now, suffice it to say that the one thing a single-screw boat cannot do as well as twin screws is handle

Figure 6-2

TWIN ENGINES *Twin-engine installations allow easier handling than singles and, usually, more horsepower than would be available from a single engine that would fit the same floor-to-ceiling space.*

easily in reverse. If total maneuverability in all directions at all times is important—as it is, for example, with a sportfisherman—you *need* twins. Otherwise you have a choice.

"What about safety and dependability?" you might ask. "Isn't it better to have two engines so you have one to get home on if one of them quits?" I'd have to answer, "possibly," but the notion of twin-screw superiority for safety purposes is largely hogwash. One well-maintained engine is far more reliable than two inadequately maintained engines, and given the time constraints we all face, it can be far more practical to keep up a single engine.

Even if you have all the time in the world, squeezing two engines into the limited space available in many pleasureboat engine compartments can make some components extremely difficult to reach. Human nature being what it is, you will be less inclined to give those hard-to-reach components the attention they deserve, regardless of their importance. Having two engines *can,* in some situations, mean you have less reliable power than you would with a single.

Then, too, some twin-screw boats simply won't go well on one. Many will (and incidentally, behavior with a single engine is a good thing to check when you sea trial a twin-screw boat), but there is no guarantee of it. Since some will only run in circles on one engine no matter what you do with the rudders, twin screws are *not* an automatic guarantee of standby power. It depends on the boat.

Twin engines are a good way to double horsepower while keeping the individual engines within the popular (and thus relatively less expensive) size range. This is also a practical way of fitting the desired horsepower into available space. True, two engines will take up more room athwartships, but inevitably they will fit the engine compartments of pleasureboats—where there's usually more width than height—better than a single engine of equivalent horsepower. Fortunately, the exception to this occurs in the very boats that can best use a large single: deep-draft displacement hulls.

Drive-System Types

The conventional drive system is what it is, and whether any particular attribute is a plus or minus depends on what you are looking for. Here's the prime "for instance": conventional drives are under the boat. This is great when you want a clean transom—say, for less interference with fishing or to moor stern-to or simply to have a larger area on which to paint the boat's name. But when you want to take your boat on and off a trailer or cruise shallow waters, underwater running gear can be a hindrance. Likewise, there are some operational trade-offs. Many of these are best left for greater in-depth discussion in the chapters on handling techniques, but the main point can be simply stated here. Conventional running gear is the least flexible system of all. Most other drive systems allow you to change their trim, the angle at which the propeller meets the water. This creates a number of possibilities ranging from changing the trim of the boat itself (in most, but not all, cases) to changing the load on the engine or engines (in every case). Though these features are desirable for many boats, they are not universally necessary, and if the conventional system didn't work basically well, it would have been replaced rather than augmented by other systems.

V-drives

These are simply conventional drives with a "kink" in them. As the name implies, the drive train makes a V, leading forward from the engine to the V gear, then turning back beneath itself to exit the hull sternward as in conventional drives. The V-drive's main function is to allow engines to be placed farther aft than they could be with conventional drives, thus allowing a larger uninterrupted cabin area forward of the engines. The drawbacks include the additional set of gears, which adds more friction to the drive train and thus reduces efficiency, and the potential balance problems that result from locating the engines aft. The former problem is very slight and not a major drawback; the latter problem can usually be overcome with trim tabs, and realistically, it can be better in some boats to have the engines in V-drive position rather than all the way back at the transom, as stern drives would probably require. I would neither choose nor reject a boat because of V-drives.

Outboards

Outboard motors were initially developed to power boats too small for conventional inboards. Indeed, until the late 1960s, a 50 hp outboard was *big,* and a 10 hp "kicker" was probably most commonplace. Interestingly, laws related to registering boats of 10 hp or more eventually made the 9.9 hp model the most universally seen outboard, as it probably is today. As of this writing, however, we also see outboards in the 300 hp neighborhood, so it's obvious that they are no longer exclusively for small boats.

Ask any old-timer about outboards, and you're sure to get a tale of woe. In the early years, and even in fairly recent history, outboards were notorious for being cranky, cantankerous, unreliable powerplants. But even if some of that history is fairly recent, it *is* history. Today's outboards are generally as reliable as any powerplant can be, and in their place are a viable alternative.

The biggest advantages outboards offer are their relatively small size and weight for the horsepower they deliver and the fact that they are usually mounted outside the boat, which leaves more interior room for people and gear. This blessing is not without its drawbacks, however. The aggravating necessity of a cut-down transom, a long-shaft lower unit, or both has been eliminated in recent years by the development of the outboard bracket. This allows a full transom—nice for keeping the boat dry in following seas or when backing down on a fish—and the bracket truly puts the whole works outside the boat. That leaves as the main drawback a cluttered transom, which for many boats (and boatmen) is a small price to pay for the added interior space the arrangement allows.

As we'll see in greater detail in the chapters on handling techniques, the ability to aim all of a propeller's thrust enables outboards to offer better cruising maneuverability than conventional drives, in which only part of the thrust is deflected by the rudder. The other side of this coin is that without propeller thrust—as when the motor is in neutral—you have limited rudder action. And at low speeds, say in docking situations, directing the thrust can lead to oversteering.

As mentioned, outboards offer the ability to adjust engine trim for maximum efficiency, though in smaller units adjustments cannot be made underway. This allows you to eliminate or at least drastically reduce some of the problems inherent in moving a relatively large object (your boat) horizontally by spinning a small object (the propeller) vertically beneath it. But some problems remain, and until recently the problems were compounded with twin outboards because both props rotated in the same direction (with conventional inboards, counter-rotating props are the norm), and the effects of torque were doubled. Now outboards in the standard horsepower range of twins come in matched sets with counter-rotating props.

This is but one more example of the ways in which manufacturers of outboard motors have been chipping away at entrenched objections. Even the fact that the motors are mostly two-cycle and need to have their lube oil mixed with the gas—a major drawback in many minds—has been addressed, especially in larger motors, by mixing systems within the motor that keep the oil and gas separate in their respective tanks until the last possible moment. These motors also use a variable mixture in which the correct amount of oil is metered automatically, its rate governed by engine speed. This eliminates the need to mix oil with the gas when you get it from the pump, and the varying mixture results in a cleaner running engine—you never have more oil in the fuel than you need.

Even smaller outboards, which call for premixing the oil, use much less oil today, so outboards are no longer the smokey stinkpots of old.

Sterndrives

If today's outboard technology had been available 30 years ago, the sterndrive might never have come about. But it wasn't, so it did. The idea was to couple the familiar inboard engine to the trimmability and steerability of the outboard's lower unit. Theoretically, it is the best of both worlds: a familiar (read: four-cycle automotive-type as opposed to the unknowns, such as reed valves inside the two-stroke outboard), reliable (as opposed to the sometimes-it-starts-sometimes-it-doesn't outboard of the late 1950s), and more powerful (big-block Chevy V-8s, for example) engine combined with all the advantages of transom power. It isn't a bad idea, and obviously, since there are still a lot of sterndrive boats being built and sold, it works. But I'm not totally convinced it is always the *best* solution. In many boats, placing a large engine or two just inside the transom is so detrimental to overall trim and balance that it takes every bit of trimmability in the drive(s) *plus* the help of tabs to get the boat on plane. A pair of lighter outboards might be better. Yet, once on plane the boats work OK, so the arrangement can't be totally wrong either.

Figure 6-3

OUTBOARD POWER   *Outboard engines, particularly when mounted on brackets, provide relatively lightweight power that doesn't intrude into usable cockpit space.*

Sterndrives were initially similar to outboards in that the twins did not always offer counter-rotating props. This has been corrected in recent years and now most sterndrives are available in matched pairs with a left-handed prop on the port drive and a right-handed one to starboard.

One particular advantage of sterndrives over outboards is a greater flexibility in the engines themselves. For example, it is now possible to couple a high-speed diesel to a heavy-duty drive unit and gain the advantages of diesel power plus trimmability. Since power trim with its ability to fine-tune the drive every moment you're underway is now a standard part of all sterndrives, the combination of high power and trimmability is a very inviting package for those seeking ultimate performance.

At cruising speeds and above, sterndrives exhibit the same improved steering control (as compared with conventional drives) seen in outboards. They also usually exhibit the same tendency to oversteer at low speeds, an idiosyncrasy that will often be exaggerated in boats particularly sensitive to the added weight in the stern (especially if both props have the same rotation). But sterndrive builders haven't been complacent, and when Volvo introduced the Duoprop drive, which has counter-rotating props on a single drive—that's right, two props, just like a torpedo—they offered a solution to several problems. My observations have been limited, but from what I've seen, Duoprop is an excellent answer. The system retains high-speed maneuverability and seems to lose the tendency to oversteer at slow speeds. Duoprop may not be *the* answer, but it certainly is a good one.

Surface Piercing

Surface piercing drives were to the 1980s what sterndrives were to the 1960s: the new kid on the block, a nautical equivalent of the better mousetrap. Yet only the execution was new; the concept goes back to the early 1900s. It took nearly 80 years for metallurgy and other technologies to catch up with the principle involved and allow a practical application.

Around the turn of the century, with the advent of internal combustion engines for boats, engineers began experimenting with propellers. Among their discoveries: Much of the applied power is lost to water friction on the shaft, strut, and propeller hub, and perhaps more important, the prop doesn't develop full thrust throughout the entire 360 degrees of its rotation, but rather produces the bulk of it in the sector from 30 to 150 degrees past top dead center (for each blade).

Among the first to attempt to use this knowledge was Albert Hickman of South Boston, Massachussetts, who tried running shafts straight out from the transom of his experimental Sea Sleds (a forerunner of the hull design seen these days in the smaller Boston Whalers). The idea worked, sort of. By allowing the propeller to break the surface (hence the name "surface piercing"), he reduced friction and gained performance. However, the water surface wasn't the only thing broken; Hickman had trouble with shafts, too. So the idea was abandoned until Howard Arneson revived it, with important modifications, in 1980.

Arneson took the basic concept and added flexibility. The external segment of the drive is connected to the internal with a universal joint and can be moved

Figure 6-4

A STERNDRIVE MODIFICATION   *Using two counter-rotating props on the same lower unit, the Duoprop drive from Volvo Penta eliminates many of the torque-related problems involved in moving a large object (the boat) through the water by rotating a small object (the prop) behind it. (Courtesy Volvo Penta)*

both vertically and horizontally by hydraulic rams similar to those on sterndrives. This adds steerability and trimmability to the equation. Offshore racers soon found that Arneson drives allowed them higher top speeds, and the drives are now widely accepted on high-performance pleasure craft as well.

Another historical note: Soon after he introduced the drive, Arneson sold the rights to gear manufacturer Borg-Warner, which began producing units for the marketplace. Not too long after that, Betty Cook (a woman who didn't even begin racing until she was 50 and a grandmother, and then quickly proved you need be neither young nor male to be a champion) introduced a similar (but sufficiently different to avoid patent infringement) system under the marque of her race-equipment team, Kaama Engineering. By 1985, Borg-Warner had ceased production of the Arneson drives, leaving the field to Kaama. As of 1989, Kaama appeared to have dropped out of the field, and Arneson, again independent, was alive and well. Verrrry interesting!

Not being one to shun controversy, I have to add a few personal opinions regarding surface piercing drives. First, I have to admit that my experience with them is limited; I have not spent as much time with them nor have I seen as many applications as I have of other systems. Yet a lot of what I have seen impressed me. For example, I have witnessed speeds of 50 mph and higher in a couple of 70-foot Magnum motoryachts. I'm not sure the same speeds could have been reached with conventional drives. Further, had the boats been set up conventionally, they would have drawn 6 feet. With the Arnesons, they only drew 3!

But I'm not sure surface piercing drives are for everyone. Back in 1983, I had the opportunity to compare two nearly identical and nearly identically powered boats. The only difference between them was that one had sterndrives, the other Kaama drives. With radar gun and stopwatch, I compared performance between them on the same day on the same waterway with the same driver. Simply stated, we did as much as we could to make the drives the only difference between the boats. What I saw was a higher top end from the surface piercing drives but better all-around performance—tighter turning radius, better acceleration (shorter time to plane), and generally easier, more responsive handling, particularly in low-speed, tight-quarters situations—from the sterndrives. I have to think that while surface piercing drives have their place, they are probably not for the beginner.

Jet Drives

Except for a number of regional builders in the Pacific Northwest who use jet drives because their boats will most likely be run in shallow, rock-strewn rivers, jets seem to show up most on either very small or very large watercraft. The waterborne scooters often called wet-bikes or Jet-Skis (which is actually Kawasaki's trade name, not a generic) use jets to eliminate the problem of the danger of a propeller. It's easy to fall off one of these "personal watercraft," and the last thing you need is to be cut up by a propeller when you do. At the other end of the spectrum, in recent years many 100-foot-plus megayachts have been powered by large diesel engines turning jet drives rather than propellers. The reasons are similar to those that caused jets to replace props in airplanes—jets are more efficient than props when it comes to moving an object rapidly through a fluid medium, whether the medium is air or water. Jets are not without their drawbacks, however, and several megayacht builders still won't use them.

Since jet drives are rarely used in boats of the size range we are discussing in this book (roughly 19 to 50 feet), you probably don't need to ponder the option. My own opinion is that the technology is still evolving and that in the future we will probably see more applications over wider ranges of boat size and type. Just as jets have never totally replaced props in the aircraft field, I seriously doubt we will ever see jets eliminating props on the water.

In today's highly packaged marketplace, you'll often find that a particular model of boat only comes one or two ways—say only with sterndrives but with a choice of a couple of different horsepower packages. That means your choice of powerplant is limited. However, you should still consider the ways in which different powerplants and drive systems fit into your boating plans. Even if a particular boat offers limited choices, different yet similar boats might offer different drive systems. It is not at all unlikely that one of the deciding factors in

Figure 6-5

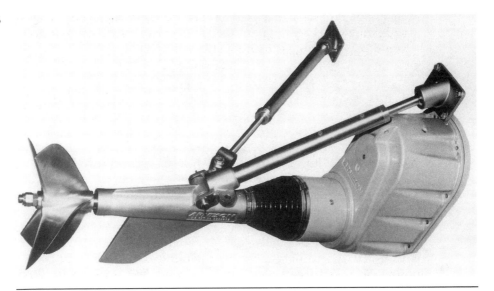

SURFACE PIERCING DRIVE   *An Arneson drive increases thrust and reduces drag by taking the prop out of the water through the least efficient portion of its rotational circle. (Courtesy Arneson Marine, Inc.)*

Figure 6-6

JET DRIVE   *Kawasaki's version of jet-driven personal watercraft has become so popular that the name Jet-Ski is now nearly generic. Jet propulsion is also often seen on much larger craft—megayachts of 90 feet and up—but rarely on anything between. (Courtesy Kawasaki)*

choosing one boat over another will be the way it is powered. Your boat has to be right for you in every way. Make sure the drive system fits your needs, or the boat as a whole may be less than totally satisfactory.

———————◆———————

7. How to Read Boat Reviews and Tests

Potential boat buyers often look to the reports published in magazines as a source of information on production powerboats. Since I have written many of them, I think I can offer some practical advice on how to read—and interpret—such articles.

First, though it will probably ruffle some feathers to do so, I have to state emphatically that I don't believe we should call them "tests." In a scientific or engineering sense, the word test implies a degree of control and repeatability that is impossible with boats. You can make a hundred different landings with the same boat at the same pier and face a hundred different sets of conditions. Wind, current, and, more important, their interaction create a nearly infinite range of variables that defies absolute repeatability.

Further, no hull is identical to the next. Even sisterships from the same mold will show discernible differences. Neither are any two propellers identical. Even if they are stamped as having the same diameter and pitch, allowable tolerances preclude precise performance comparisons unless they are specifically calibrated (and those you buy off the shelf are not) . So testing a boat is not like running a car on a test track, using known tires inflated to a known pressure on a surface of known quality and double-checking results by dragging a "fifth wheel." You simply can't test boats as you do cars!

By that, do I mean to imply that the reports have no value? Not at all. They can be extremely beneficial. It's just that you should understand what boat reports are not before you can appreciate what they are; you have to know what not to look for before you can see what's there.

Don't look for data chiseled in stone. Although some magazines (including those I have written for) make a big deal out of the thoroughness of their testing, it's really a matter of smoke and mirrors. Performance figures, speed curves, fuel consumption, and the other hard data articles often contain should be accepted as valid—for the subject boat, under the conditions prevailing at the time of the "test." They should not be taken as absolutes and definitely should not be projected as such onto a boat you're considering unless *that particular boat* (not merely the same model) was the one tested. Though "test" figures should be close to what you might experience with a similar boat, you cannot expect to duplicate them exactly. If you read that the "Zipper 425" hits 35 mph at wide-open throttle (WOT), and the one you just bought tops out at 33, you shouldn't feel short-changed. Neither should you feel terribly special if yours shows 36. Just remember that we can only give ballpark figures, and you'll be OK.

Figure 7-1

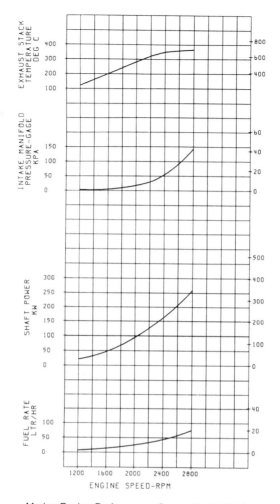

Marine Engine Performance Curve, Model 3208

THE APPLICATION OF POWER *Boating magazines often go to great lengths to "test" boats' performance, but the truth is that a properly powered boat with the right components in its drive train will nearly mirror the engine manufacturer's dynamometer-derived performance curves. (Courtesy Caterpillar Inc.)*

Don't look for comparisons. Apples and oranges are more alike than many outwardly similar boats. Once in a while a story will concentrate on the similarities and differences of a certain type of craft as produced by different builders, but for the most part each report is about a particular boat and that boat only. How it may or may not compare with others is beyond the scope of a reasonable article.

Filling a Need

When I first began to write boating articles, my editor gave me this advice: "Discover the niche the boat was designed to fill, then concentrate on how well the boat does what it was intended to." To this day, I try to follow that advice, and I still believe that the only valid comparison to use in a boat report is the real world boat against the boat's intentions. Anything else is speculation.

Don't look for major negatives. There are reasons for this. I can only speak for myself, but the biggest to me is (to paraphrase Will Rogers) that I've never met a boat I didn't like. Well, let me amend that. In more than a dozen years of writing boat reports, I've seen only two boats that didn't have far more positive attributes than negative. In both instances I was aboard a prototype, and the truth is, all parties involved were guilty of one-upmanship. The builders (two different companies were involved) let us examine not-yet-finished prototypes in the hope of getting early publicity, and the magazine was out to scoop the competition. In both cases, I felt the only fair thing to do was write nothing—and told the builders why there would be no story. In both instances the builders ultimately agreed that the boat had more negative than positive characteristics and decided that to try to correct the situation would involve throwing good money after bad. Neither boat was ever released as a production model.

No boat is perfect, and I always try to find places where improvement is warranted and point them out to the reader. Such a search is never impossible, but it is becoming more difficult. These days, builders seem to wait until all the developmental problems are solved before they'll let us aboard, and many smart builders willingly sacrifice early press coverage while they work out most of the production problems as well—which means waiting until they've launched hull number 4 or 5. With all of the bugs thus eliminated, the boats we review come as close to being perfect as anything produced by the hand of man can be.

There's another big reason we don't dwell on negatives: We can't spend enough time with a boat to discover all of them, and there isn't space in the magazine to go into the extensive detail that would be required to give a truly in-depth report.

Back in the late 1970s, I was with the late and lamented *Motorboat* magazine (a name which has since been revived) and had the responsibility of developing the structure for its report program. Based on my experience as a surveyor, I worked up a list of over 150 individual items that we rated on a scale of one to ten whenever we examined a boat. The items were grouped under electrical system, hull and superstructure, living space, and so on, and each group received a combined rating. Our inspection was as close to a survey as we could get. Further, to reduce subjectivity to a minimum, each boat was inspected by two of us working independently. We then compared and averaged our results for the final report. But most important, we also spent three or four days actually *using* the boat as it was intended to be used. We'd get a few couples together and take cruising boats on a cruise. We went fishing with fishing boats. In short, we got familiar enough with each boat to learn what worked and what didn't. The reports reflected this.

However, when the *Power and Motoryacht* editor asked me about developing a similar boat-test program for that magazine, I had to advise against it. Quite honestly, it simply was not cost-effective—two people tied up four to six days on one article isn't practical. Nor would it be space-effective in print, since the information thus generated would require more pages than can realistically be devoted to a single boat, especially in the publishing world as it exists today. (When I started writing boat reports they were about 2,500 words. A few years ago we cut back to 2,000, and now many run around 1,600. You can see the trend.)

Finally, we have to admit that boat reports are, to a degree, for the dreamer in all of us and as such tend more toward "show biz" than pure journalism. For every reader who gleans a report for facts about a boat he's considering, many more read it to enjoy vicariously a boat they will never own. Because no boat can be everything we want and few of us can afford a different boat for every need, we buy the boat that suits us best and merely read about the rest. This reality precludes a "Consumer Reports" type of coverage, which would presume that every report is for a potential buyer.

So what *is* a boat report? I believe its objective is to reflect upon the unique qualities of each boat and evaluate these as fairly and honestly as possible. In the final analysis, every report is generated by a human being writing about something which, by its very nature, involves a lot of emotionality, so inevitably there will be personal bias. We boat testers try to be objective, but we can't help but be influenced by our own likes and dislikes. To counter this, you should read a lot of reviews and compare what you read with what you see at marinas, in dealers' showrooms, and at boatshows. You'll learn which writers have views similar to your own. Just as you might rush to see a movie panned by a critic whose opinion is generally opposite yours, you can interpret boat reviewers' reports in the same light.

At the same time, you should develop your own standards and be honest about your own likes and dislikes. If, for instance, you can't stand spinach, a restaurant review raving about chicken Florentine won't impress you at all. With experience, you'll interpret boat reports in the same fashion.

Boat reports are a great way for all of us to enjoy boats we would otherwise never get to see, and they are a fine way to become acquainted with some boats we *may* eventually see. In this respect, they are an excellent vehicle to use in the early stages of shopping. But don't let the printed word influence you too much. When you are shopping for a boat, you're looking for the boat that's right for you. The pictures may be pretty, the words may ring with praise, but it's the real boat in the real world that has to suit you. Learn to be your own reviewer.

———————◆———————

8. Twenty Questions to Codify Boat Selection

Let's make the process of boat selection simpler by encapsulating it in twenty questions you should ask yourself before or as you look. Write down the answers so you'll be sure not to overlook anything.

1. How will I most often use the boat? Be realistic. Don't talk yourself into an impractical boat simply because it has desirable features. Remember boat-buying rule number 2, "Your boat should make your favorite on-the-water activities easy." I might also add, fun. Look for the boat that will suit *your* intended uses, and don't settle for anything else. And remember, you can't find the boat best suited to your needs until you define your needs.

2. Where will I use it? The answer is going to influence many things about your boat: its size, powerplant (remember, outboards and sterndrives are generally better for trailered boats), the amount of beef in its construction, the amount and type of shelter aboard, and more. Be realistic at the outset, and you'll be happier down the line.

3. How much time do I have to use it? It's easy to overestimate available time when you are excited about buying a boat. Time shrinks in the real world, and there's nothing worse than having a boat that needs more time and attention than you can give it.

All boats need attention, mostly in the form of simple routine maintenance, but some need more than others. Likewise, some boats need more attention before you leave the dock and when you get back. The less time you have, the more important it is to have a simple, no-frills boat. Do you think oiled teak covering boards are the saltiest looking cosmetic treatment a boat can have? Get them, if you have time to keep them oiled. If your time is limited, you'd be better off with surfaces that only ask for washing.

Back before I got my priorities straight and decided it was better to work all the time on someone else's boat than to work five days ashore to get two on a boat of my own, I made it a rule never to accept an invitation that would keep me ashore on a weekend during the boating season. Friends often felt snubbed until they experienced one weekend of cruising themselves. Then, usually, they would envy me for spending *every* weekend on my boat. It worked for me, but I'm not so sure it would for everyone. Be serious in your estimates of available time and plan your boat accordingly.

4. Where will I keep it when I'm not using it? If you are new to boating, this question might seem irrelevant. But it won't be long before you realize that slip space is often as scarce as virgins in Times Square, and when you find space, you'll discover it can be as precious as platinum. Space *is* available, even if you have to suffer through a couple of years on a waiting list to get it. My point is, don't go out and buy a 40-foot cabin cruiser, even if it suits all your other needs perfectly, unless you have a place to park a 40-footer when you're not using it. If

Figure 8-1

TRAILERABLE BOAT *Trailerable boats offer many practical advantages, not least of which are that you can keep your boat at home and have an almost unlimited choice of boating areas. (Courtesy Calkins)*

it's going to have to sit in your driveway, it's going to have to fit in your driveway (and be trailerable to boot).

5.   Will it be *my* boat or a family boat? Since boating is a perfect sport for the whole family to enjoy together, maybe the question needn't be asked. But boating isn't always for everyone, and it just may be that what you need is the perfect boat for occasional use by you and some fishing buddies rather than a larger, more luxurious vessel your spouse and kids could enjoy on a regular basis. If you plan to include your family, however, make sure the boat is meant for a family. Comfort can be subjective; let your family help judge what is comfortable.

6.   Is the answer to question 1 in line with question 5? Could be you've already covered this one. But it won't hurt to double-check. In listing needs by use, have you thought of everyone who will regularly be using the boat with you? Some compromise may be necessary here; the boat that best fills most of your criteria may not suit everyone in the family equally well. Better to consider all needs and compromise accordingly than to spoil the fun for other family members.

7.   How much can I spend to buy it? A wag once described a boat as "a hole in the water surrounded by fiberglass into which one pours money." As with many jests, there's an element of truth in it. The purchase is just the beginning, so don't blow your budget up front. Like all rules, this one can be bent slightly, but don't bend it too far or you'll break yourself rather than the rule.

8.   How much can I spend on operation? Most operational expenses are directly related to the size and type of boat you buy. Marina and yard charges, for example, are usually based on overall length. While many costs are fixed—dockage, insurance, hauling, and winter storage if you are a seasonal boatman, for example—fuel and some maintenance costs will vary with use. Obviously, the more you use your boat, the more hours the fixed costs are spread over and the less the cost per hour. Still, your choice of boat will influence operational costs; a gas guzzler will burn more fuel per hour than the more economical low-horsepower single-screw trawler. This doesn't make the trawler better, it only means that you have to face and plan for long-term expenses. Check with marinas and yards to determine current costs and figure accordingly. This may help you determine how large a boat you can afford. Find out about insurance—different types of boats carry different rates. In short, be sure to include a realistic appraisal of *all* operating costs when you make up your boating budget.

9.   How much can I spend on maintenance? Maintenance costs depend to a degree on the size of the boat but even more on its simplicity. The more fancy stuff you have aboard, the more time and money it will take to keep everything shipshape and working properly. If you want to spend your time and money enjoying the boat rather than taking care of it, keep it simple.

One way to save on maintenance is to spend time instead of money—do the work yourself. And that brings up the next question.

10.   Is do-it-yourself maintenance practical for me? If you resent the hours spent on maintenance, be prepared to pay others to work on your boat when you can't be there. But perhaps you'll find, as many have, that maintaining your boat can be a big part of the enjoyment. If this is the case, you may even discover that when other engagements prevent you from taking the whole day to go boating, you can still spend a morning or afternoon on needed maintenance.

The more work you do yourself, the better you'll know your boat and its systems and the less you'll be upset should something go awry underway. Of course this presupposes that you have the requisite knowledge, but as your boating experience grows, there's no reason why your maintenance knowledge can't grow with it.

11.   How big a boat do I *need*? Bigger is not necessarily better, but you do need a boat large enough to be comfortable for all concerned. A boat that's too small won't be fun. When you examine all the elements—purchase price, operational costs, and so forth, *plus* the needs of your family—you may decide that a larger simple boat will fit your needs better than a smaller fancy one at the same bottom line.

12.   How big a boat can I handle? Generally speaking, the bigger the boat, the more knowledge and experience you need to handle it properly. The reason

Figure 8-2

TEAK TRIM   *In today's world of plastic boats, a bit of teak—such as the step and handrail we see on this Maxum—can add a touch of natural warmth. Just remember: Wood, even as forgiving a variety as teak, demands more maintenance than plastic.*

is simple: Larger boats react more slowly. That means more planning ahead on the part of the skipper. The less experience you have, the tougher it is to plan ahead.

The 80-foot boat I'm currently skippering takes about 30 to 40 seconds to react to a change of controls. Not only do I have to know what I want to happen, I have to decide what adjustment will achieve the desired result nearly a minute ahead of time so as to initiate the proper action at the proper time. I don't think I could do it if I hadn't been running big boats for a number of years. You can learn with the boat no matter what its size, but you'll have an easier time of it if you don't bite off too much too soon.

13.   What's the biggest boat that suits all of the above? This is your upper limit. You don't have to get one that big, and you might find something smaller that meets all your needs best, but you do have to set limits. Decide what you can accept as your biggest boat *at this time*, then live with your decision no matter how appealing some larger boat might be.

14.   What's the smallest boat that suits all of the above? Again, you may well buy something larger, but you have to define your limits in order to narrow your choices. Just as you might pass by the exciting two-seater sports car when you're really in the market for a station wagon, you have to bypass boats too small for your current purposes if you want to make your search realistic and practical.

Figure 8-3

BOATS ON DRY LAND   *Though boats commonly stay in the water at all times, marinas in many parts of the country now offer dry-stack stowage (background) to get more boats into a given area. Usually, it only takes an advance phone call to have your boat in the water and waiting for you when you arrive.*

15.   What features are most important? Remembering rule number 1, "Every boat is a compromise," you have to know which features are least negotiable before you can begin making deals with yourself. The best way to handle this is simply to list everything you are looking for in a boat and then arrange the items in order of descending importance.

16.   What features are least important? This should be fairly easy. Just don't be hasty. It's entirely possible that some of these least important features are attainable, but you can't count on it, so don't list anything that isn't truly expendable.

17.   What features are absolutely necessary? This again is simply a matter of drawing a line—in this case between those things you really need and those you only want very much. Though the principle of compromise is to give up what you want least to gain what you want most, sometimes in the real world you have to give up what you would want more to gain what you want most. Be very clear in your own mind as to which features are positively *not* negotiable.

18.   What features are absolutely unnecessary? The point in even including these items (since they most likely won't be a part of your boat) is simply to help you get priorities completely straight in your mind. If it isn't on your list, you won't know where it fits into your priorities.

Here's a suggestion: After you have made your initial list of desirable features, assign each item to a category from 1 to 5. Use 5 for things you must have, 4 for those you would like very much, 3 for those that would be nice, 2 for those that are expendable, and 1 for those you can definitely do without. Then rearrange and start shopping with full confidence that you know exactly what you are looking for.

Again: Too many 5s on your list, and it just won't work. That's not to say the list must be perfectly balanced, but if everything on your list is a "must have" you leave yourself no room to compromise.

19.   Have I found the best dealer? This question can be far more important than you might imagine. In fact, finding the right dealer can be more critical than finding the right boat.

Because nothing made by the hand of man is perfect, you have to face the truth that your wonderful new boat is going to give you some problems. It will when it's new; it will after you've owned it awhile. It will, period. The pleasures of owning a powerboat far outweigh the problems, however, and this is especially true if you have a cooperative and understanding dealer. A good dealer will do his utmost to minimize your problems and maximize your fun. But you must also be a good customer. The customer-dealer relationship is often a matter of chemistry, which means the right dealer for you is not necessarily the right dealer for your best friend.

There are some general guidelines, however. The best dealer will have a strong service department with the tools, parts, and knowledgeable mechanics it takes to get your service work done quickly and correctly, handling everything from warranty work to routine maintenance. But a good service department will be busy, so smart dealers pay attention to their own customers first—one good reason not to look only at the purchase bottom line. If you shop entirely by sales price, expecting to get another dealer to do the service work, be prepared to stand in line behind the dealer's regular customers every time. For similar reasons, the best dealer will be close to your boating area even if you can get a seemingly better deal farther down the road.

The best dealer will be more concerned with helping you find the right boat than in merely making a sale. He wants to sell you a lot of boats, not just one, because chances are that if you enjoy boating, you won't stop with one boat. After a few years you'll want something else—most likely something bigger. (That's why in question 13 I made the point about determining the biggest boat that suits you *at this time;* eventually you will answer the question differently.) Boatbuilders recognize the probability of this progression and keep adding to the top of their line. In the late 1970s, for instance, the largest Sea Ray was a 36-footer, and the biggest factory Hatteras, 77 feet (though some dealers specialize in making customized stretch models that are longer than standard). By the late 1980s Sea Ray had gotten up to 50 feet and Hatteras to 120!

A truly smart dealer knows that you won't want to move up to something bigger unless you like nearly everything about the boat you have now except its size. If he steers you wrong in the beginning, that first boat may be the only one you ever get. Some dealers are happy with that single sale. The good ones look ahead and cultivate long-term customer relationships.

20.   Have I found the best deal? Unless the boat meets the criteria you have outlined for yourself, the answer to this question is "no"; no matter what incentives a dealer may offer, you don't have a good deal if the boat isn't right to begin with. But let's assume for the moment that the boat is essentially ideal and take a look at what makes a good deal better and what you can do to make it best.

Shop around. Sure, I said the dealer with the lowest price is not necessarily the best place to buy your boat, and I'll stand by that advice. But until you see what the marketplace has to offer, you can't begin to negotiate. And you should negotiate, provided you're realistic. The dealer with the great service department and in-depth parts inventory will probably have a higher overhead than the dealer who sells but doesn't service boats. Don't expect to get the same price from both. But by knowing what the lowest price may be, you'll have a better idea of what an acceptable price should be from the dealer you'd rather do business with. Even the best dealer will usually start out asking more than he expects, just so he has room to come down a bit. It's the nature of the business.

Consider the cost of money along with the cost of the boat. A boat is a major purchase, so you will probably be financing it with a consumer loan. Lenders appreciate boat buyers, who, for the most part, are good customers. Using the boat as collateral, you can borrow a large chunk of the purchase price.

Though pleasureboating has long since ceased to be the sole province of the very rich, it is still a luxury. If you have the discretionary income to be able to afford boating, you probably have the savvy to shop for your boat loan as carefully as you shop for the boat itself. So I'll just add the reminder.

Popular production boats are much like automobiles in that they depreciate quickly when new. This has been aggravated in recent years by an excess of demand over supply of popular new boats (which keeps their prices up), coupled with excess supply in the used-boat market (which holds their value down). You should ensure if possible that you owe no more on your boat than you could get if you were to sell it tomorrow. A dealer may be reluctant to let you in on how much you're going to lose to initial depreciation, but you should try to ascertain it nevertheless. Otherwise, when you prepare to trade up to something bigger in a year or two, you'll discover that not only does your boat not have any trade-in value, you might actually have to *add* cash just to pay off the note and satisfy the lien—particularly if you made little or no down payment to begin with.

———————◆———————

PART

TWO

THE WHYS OF
POWERBOAT
HANDLING

———◆———

9. Why Boats Don't Behave like Cars

It happens to nearly every boating neophyte. You're sitting alongside a pier or float. When the lines have been cast off and you're ready to get underway, you do as you would with a car at a curb: turn the steering wheel away from the pier, put the boat in gear, and advance the throttle gently. You expect your boat to glide away from the pier as smoothly as your car glides away from the curb. But it doesn't. Instead of the bow swinging gracefully away from the pier, the stern swings *into* it with a thump. Surprise! You've just learned lesson number one in boathandling: Despite having a motor, throttle, and steering wheel, powerboats do not behave like cars. Let's see *why* they don't, and perhaps more important, let's find out how boats *do* behave.

In a car, your steering action is in the front wheels. (These days, the drive power often is, too.) Aim the front, and the rear end follows. In a boat, your motive power *and* steering control are both in the stern. Remember this if you remember nothing else: When you steer a boat, nothing happens until the stern swings. Nothing! That's the *what*. But let's examine the *whys*, because it's usually easier to understand actions if we know what causes them.

We'll begin with single screw. One engine, one propeller, one rudder. And since it offers a good basis of understanding as well as a standard against which we can later compare other systems, we'll start with conventional underwater gear. In the following examples, I'll be talking about the actions of a *right-handed* propeller—one that turns clockwise in forward gear when viewed from astern. In all cases the actions of a left-handed wheel would be opposite. We'll also pretend for the moment that outside forces such as wind and current don't exist and look only at the actions of the boat itself.

How a Boat Is Steered

As a powerboat moves forward, a stream of water, called the "discharge screw current," is forced aft by the propeller (Figure 9-1). We steer the boat by deflecting this current (as well as the apparent current created by the boat's movement through the water) with a rudder (Figure 9-2). If there's no flow across the rudder, there is no control, which is why you cannot steer a boat that is drifting.

Most modern powerboats use a balanced rudder—that is, one with part of its blade forward of the rudderpost—so that more of the screw current can be deflected when the rudder is turned. Even with a balanced rudder, however, some of the screw current misses the turned blade and is not deflected. This undeflected thrust tends to push a boat straight ahead despite the angled rudder and is another reason your boat won't behave quite the way your car does when you turn the steering wheel.

The ease with which a boat turns depends on the location and size of its rudder in relation to the location and size of its propeller. It also depends on engine speed: Rudder action increases with an increase in engine rpm because the screw current increases.

Figure 9-1

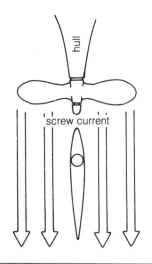

DISCHARGE SCREW CURRENT

Figure 9-2

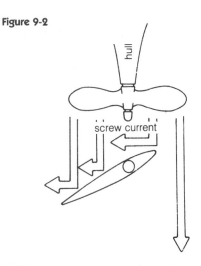

STEERING FORCES

A boat going astern has no screw current passing over the rudder (Figure 9-3). What turning power there is must be supplied by the rudder's movement through the water. Thus it can be extremely difficult, if not impossible, to steer a single-screw boat in reverse.

The Forces at Work

One of the first things we discover about single-screw boats is that with the rudder amidships (centered), a boat with a right-handed screw will have a tendency to veer slightly to port. In Figure 9-4 we see the reason why. In addition to the main thrust provided by the discharge screw current, another force, usually called "side thrust," comes into play. Discussions about the causes of side thrust will probably keep dockside sea lawyers busy for years; every experienced boatman has his pet theory. It may be that the propeller blades swing in a denser fluid and with greater efficiency in the bottom hemisphere (moving starboard to port) than the top hemisphere (moving port to starboard) of each revolution. This induces the stern to "claw" to starboard and thus the bow to fall off to port. A more important factor, however, is that the propeller shaft is inclined from the horizontal plane as it leaves the hull, and thus the propeller is not square to the water surface, a condition we'll reexamine in Chapter 11 on "Transom Power." Regardless of its causes, side thrust is real and is one of the forces we must deal with in handling a powerboat.

Momentum is another. Boats don't have brakes, and even after you back off on the throttle and put the gear lever in neutral, momentum will keep a boat moving forward. We'll deal with this in greater detail later; for now let's just affirm that in boat handling, "no brakes!" is almost as important as "nothing happens until the stern swings."

Figure 9-3

Figure 9-4

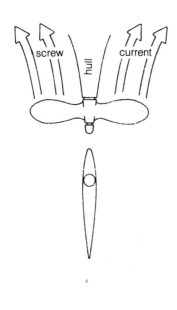

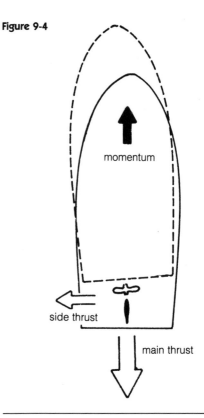

ABSENCE OF STEERING CONTROL IN REVERSE GEAR

THE FORCES AT WORK: WITH HEADWAY, RUDDER AMIDSHIP

Momentum also affects the way a boat turns. Since it is not following its front wheels as a car does, a boat moves forward at least slightly before initiating its turn. Couple this with the stern swing, and you can see that putting a boat precisely where you want it takes a different approach from putting a car where you want it.

Figure 9-5 shows what happens in a left turn underway. The stern swings to starboard (stern swing is always the initial action), and from a combination of forces—momentum and undeflected screw current—the boat advances slightly as it turns. Note also that stern swing is greater than the resulting bow swing; in effect, the boat pivots around a point which is about one-third of a boat length abaft the bow. Even though you are turning left, you need ample clearance on your right.

The exact location of the pivot point depends on hull design and varies from boat to boat. It also depends somewhat on speed and in a given boat will change slightly with throttle setting. With practice and experience, you'll learn where your boat's pivot point is and just how it moves when you advance or retard the throttle. Viewed from a different perspective, you'll learn the clearances you need to swing the boat around without hitting anything in the process.

Figure 9-5

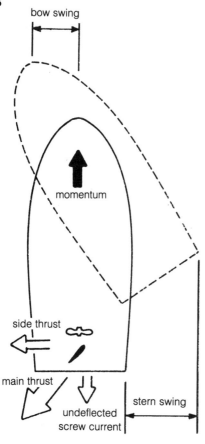

THE FORCES AT WORK: WITH HEADWAY, LEFT RUDDER

Figure 9-6

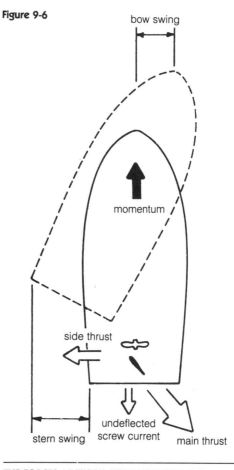

THE FORCES AT WORK: WITH HEADWAY, RIGHT RUDDER

Another thing you'll learn in a single-screw boat is that right turns are different from left turns. In Figure 9-6 we see that turning right, against the side thrust, lessens stern swing and as a result causes a broader turn.

How to Stop without Brakes

Because boats don't have brakes, to stop you must create an opposing force to arrest your forward motion. The solution is to put the screw in reverse. In Figure 9-7, we see what happens when you do. The boat stops after some advance, the extent of which depends on several factors including the weight of the boat, its speed at the time, and how much power you apply in reverse.

When you use reverse to stop, you will discover another phenomenon. Side thrust in reverse is not only the opposite of side thrust in forward, it is stronger! Again, the reasons are too numerous and complex for discussion here, but the result is worth emphasizing: Side thrust when going astern will always be

Figure 9-7

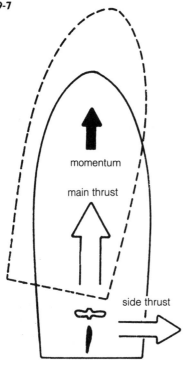

momentum

main thrust

side thrust

Figure 9-8

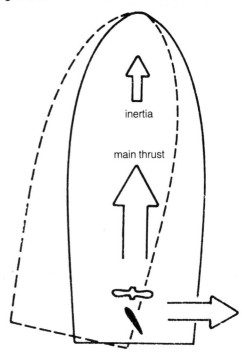

inertia

main thrust

THE FORCES AT WORK: WITH HEADWAY, RUDDER AMIDSHIP, ENGINE BACKING

THE FORCES AT WORK: DEAD IN THE WATER, POWER APPLIED ASTERN, RIGHT RUDDER

stronger (at equivalent rpm) than side thrust going ahead. The stern will most likely swing to port as you come to a halt, and it is in fact very difficult to hold a single-screw boat straight at such times.

Whatever problems side thrust may cause when you are trying to stop pale in comparison with what happens when you try to back up. In Figure 9-8 we see the actions of a right-handed single-screw boat when you apply reverse while dead in the water. First, the stern swings to port—often markedly. Then sternway develops. One thing is for certain: The rudder has little effect until considerable sternway develops. The reason, of course, is that lacking screw current across it, the rudder can't do much until sternway creates a boat-motion current across it. That's why steerageway astern requires a much higher speed than steerageway forward.

Later we'll see how we can make these inevitable actions work for us. But in the meantime, let's see what we can do to eliminate them.

———————◆———————

10. The Twin-Screw Advantage

There are several ways to overcome the drawbacks inherent in single-screw conventional drive, and before we're through, we'll examine them all. But first, let's see what happens when we stick with conventional drives and add a second screw.

Though it is by no means the only way, the most common twin-screw practice uses counter-rotating props with a left-handed screw on the port side and a right-handed screw to starboard. What we get from this is in effect an absence of side thrust. It's still there, of course, but because one of the causes of side thrust is the torque (rotational force) from a spinning propeller, counter-rotating props cancel each other's side thrust. Figure 10-1 shows counter-rotating twin screws in forward gear. In the absence of other forces (that is, disregarding wind and current), a twin-screw boat with both props in forward gear will go straight ahead when you put the rudders amidship. Gone is the single-screw tendency to veer to one side. Also gone is the difference between left and right turns.

However pleasant this may be, the big difference is seen with the props in reverse (Figure 10-2). Side thrust is still greater when a prop is set astern—you can't change that. But with *both* props astern, the cancelling effect of counter-rotation allows the boat to back straight. And since the overpowering side thrust we saw in the single-screw situation is now tamed by the counteracting side thrust from the other prop, a twin-screw boat will usually follow its rudders in reverse much sooner than will a single-screw boat.

Utilizing the power of side thrust, it is possible to work some twin-screw maneuvers without even considering rudder action. Indeed, when we get to specific boathandling situations later in the book, I'll suggest that you initially forget the steering wheel and work only with the clutches—propeller forces alone are that strong. When maneuvering with clutches and throttles, it helps to think of a big "X" superimposed on your boat with the base at the console and the

Figure 10-1

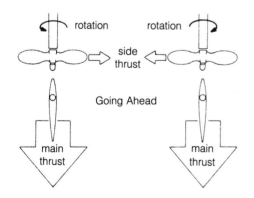

THE FORCES AT WORK: TWIN SCREW, BOTH ENGINES AHEAD, RUDDERS AMIDSHIP

Figure 10-2

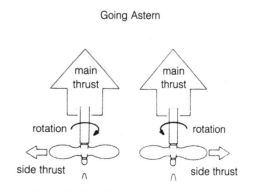

THE FORCES AT WORK: TWIN SCREWS, BOTH ENGINES ASTERN

Turning completely around is a classic twin-screw maneuver. While this move has some practical applications in itself, it is the factors which make it possible that lend to the greater maneuverability of a twin-screw boat.

top at the bow (Figure 10-3). This will help remind you that putting either engine in forward gear swings the bow toward the opposite side (left turn with starboard engine, for example) and the stern toward the same side.

Throttle and clutch maneuvering can produce some neat results. For example, you can spin a twin-screw boat around quite nicely by "splitting" the clutches; that is, by putting one prop ahead and the other astern (Figure 10-4). If you also bring the rudders into play—for example, using right rudder along with the port engine ahead and starboard engine astern—the boat will usually turn in a much tighter circle (Figure 10-5), and often within its own length.

However, when you set the rudders *opposite* the split clutches—in this case left rudder with port engine ahead—an amazing thing can happen: The boat slides sideways (Figure 10-6). I say "can" rather than "will" because the ultimate action depends on a number of factors including the relative placement of the rudders within the discharge screw current and the proportionate force of side thrust for a particular boat. Basically the propeller forces tend to push the bow to starboard while the angled rudders tend to push the stern to starboard. If the forces balance, both ends go to starboard—i.e., the boat slides. In actual practice, engine speeds may have to be adjusted for optimum effect; sometimes one engine or the other (usually the one astern, since side thrust astern is stronger) has to go in and out of gear to balance the thrusts, and often the boat "walks" rather than slides sideways. But unless you are trying to move the boat directly into an opposing wind (which is rarely possible), the boat usually *will move sideways* with little movement ahead or back.

Figure 10-3

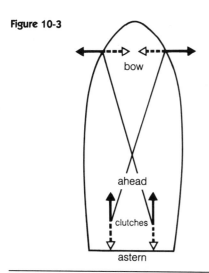

STEERING WITH THE CLUTCHES *Imagine a huge X superimposed on your boat to remind yourself that moving either clutch control ahead induces the bow to turn toward the opposite side. Throwing the starboard engine into forward gear, for example, induces a turn to the left.*

Figure 10-4

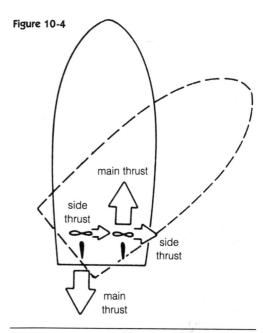

THE FORCES AT WORK: ONE ENGINE AHEAD, ONE ASTERN

Figure 10-5

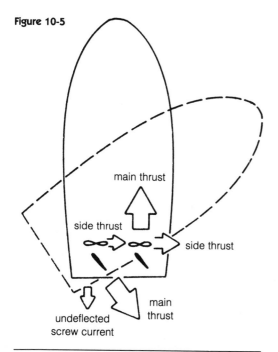

THE FORCES AT WORK: ONE ENGINE AHEAD, ONE ASTERN, RUDDERS SET "WITH" THE TURN

Figure 10-6

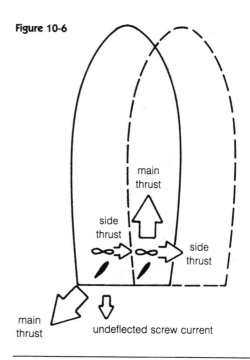

THE FORCES AT WORK: ONE ENGINE AHEAD, ONE ASTERN, RUDDERS SET "AGAINST" THE TURN

1. *With both engines astern (rudders amidship for least drag) the boat backs straight. Unless there is influence from outside forces, the boat will back as straight as you wish for as long as you wish.*

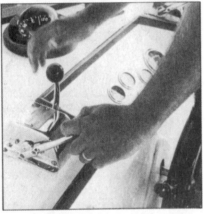

2. *Turns are best accomplished without touching the steering wheel by simply taking one engine out of gear. The offset main thrust will swing the stern toward the out-of-gear side.*

3. *To tighten the turn, put the out-of-gear engine in forward. Then, before the boat is lined up on the intended course, put the engine back in neutral. As the boat nearly approaches the course, put the engine astern and your turn will be completed as you once again back straight. Just how soon to shift is a variable, and developing the proper timing is a part of learning your own boat's responses. In time, you will feel that the boat is an extension of your hands, as it moves ahead or astern or turns in any direction forward or back simply by your moving the clutch controls.*

We'll look at specific twin-screw handling techniques in a later chapter, but now let's examine other ways of overcoming the problems of the single scew.

———————◆———————

11 • Transom Power

We just saw one way to overcome the problems associated with single-screw conventional drives: Add a counter-rotating prop. Another solution is to move the motive power out from under the boat and hang it off the transom. While there are minor operational differences between outboards, sterndrives, and surface-piercing drives, they are not important enough to warrant a distinction at this point, so we will lump the drives together under the rubric "transom power." And since outboards and sterndrives are seen in far greater numbers, we will concentrate primarily on their behavior.

In some ways, transom power offers a *big* advantage over conventional drive systems. A single, properly trimmed outdrive (a synonym for sterndrive) or outboard lower unit exhibits little of the side thrust behavior of single-screw conventional drive. Better still, turning the steering wheel redirects the entire discharge screw current, thus eliminating the problems that result from the undeflected screw current of conventional drives (Figures 11-1 and 11-2). The result is much better maneuverability—tighter turns, less tendency to veer, straight stops, easy steering in reverse, etc. However, we see much of this improvement only at cruising speeds. The downside is that lacking a true rudder, a transom-powered boat gliding along under momentum alone is not as easy to steer as a conventional inboard. Yet when you apply power at low speed, the totally directed discharge current has a bigger effect, and that can lead to *over*steering. Compounding the problem, most transom-powered boats have planing hulls that are not always on their best behavior in the low-speed displacement mode; they perform better when going fast. The bottom line is that transom-powered boats can be very touchy at low speeds as you alternate between too little steering action when the propeller is not engaged and too much when you put it in gear. You must learn by experience exactly how gentle you have to be with the throttle and steering wheel to get the actions you want during low-speed maneuvers.

On the whole, these drawbacks can be relatively unimportant in light of the positive control you have at cruising speeds. And the ability to adjust transom drive(s) to optimum trim is a *huge* advantage over conventional drives with a planing hull.

Keeping Trim

One of the causes of side thrust in conventional drives is the angle at which the propeller meets the water (caused in turn by the angle at which the shaft leaves the hull). This changes the effective pitch of the blades so their ability to convert torque (rotary force) into forward propulsion is not constant throughout the circle of rotation. As I pointed out in Chapter 6, the greatest action occurs between 30 and 150 degrees of rotation, so a right-handed wheel has more bite on its starboard side. The imbalances contribute to side thrust. Because you can adjust (trim) a transom-mounted drive unit so that the plane of the prop revolutions is exactly perpendicular to the line of forward motion, this problem can be eliminated.

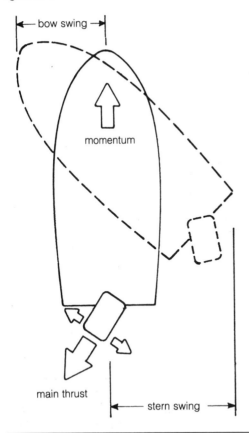

THE FORCES AT WORK: TRANSOM POWER *Because the whole drive unit turns, there is no undeflected screw current and therefore all the thrust serves to turn the boat.*

THE FORCES AT WORK: DEAD IN THE WATER, POWER APPLIED ASTERN *Backing with transom power is much easier than backing a single-screw inboard, because side thrust is manageable and the screw current is fully directable.*

Though some side thrust remains (a product of torque), it can be counteracted by adjusting the mini-rudder or fin usually found beneath the anticavitation plate just above the prop (Figure 11-3). When set correctly, this small fin lets you go straight with the main "rudder" (i.e., the drive unit) set amidships. The drawback here is that the fin works best at just one speed, providing less corrective action when you go faster or slower. You have to decide what speed you want that to be (the usual choice is normal cruising speed) and adjust the fin accordingly.

While the results are less readily apparent in higher powered outboards or sterndrives with power-assisted steering, outboards with simple rope steering systems will quickly tell you if you have the trim set right. A properly trimmed drive system will hold its course quite well even if you take your hands off the

Figure 11-3

THE MINI-RUDDER *Located under the anticavitation plate of most transom drive units, the mini-rudder helps counterbalance side thrust. It is adjustable, because side thrust is a result of both propeller forces and hull forces and thus changes from boat to boat. When the tab is set at the proper angle, an otherwise properly trimmed boat will maintain a steady course by itself.*

steering wheel. If the boat won't stay on course or if you have to fight the wheel, you need to adjust the trim. You can also see the effects of improper trim in boats with power steering; some turns will be easier to hold than others. It's just not quite as obvious as it is with a looser steering system.

Adjusting the mini-rudder on the anticavitation plate is one of two ways you can affect trim. The other is by setting the vertical angle of the drive unit, and while I do not wish to diminish the importance of the former, the latter is perhaps more critical. While improper adjustment of the trim fin can make a boat hard to steer, improper vertical trim can adversely affect everything from the way the boat rides to fuel economy and even its speed. As I said in Chapter 3, all planing hulls deliver noticeably better performance when they are trimmed correctly, and this holds true for *all* planing hulls, not just performance craft.

Sterndrives and modern large outboards offer the advantage of continuous power trim. This means you can adjust the angle of trim in nearly infinite increments throughout the available range and at any time to respond to changing conditions. Smaller outboards (as well as most older ones of any horsepower) can be trimmed also but only through a "pin-in-hole" arrangement that lacks the range of angles and the ability to make adjustments underway. In this configuration you have to put the pin through the set of holes that offers optimum trim for the way you use the boat most of the time. Any drastic change in load or basic operating speed will call for a change in setting. Because you can't make constant adjustments underway, you must resort to other methods (shifting the load within the boat, for example) or stop the motor to move the pin.

Optimum Trim

Ideally, the boat will run on its lines, and the prop will be perpendicular to forward motion; i.e., the drive unit will be exactly vertical (Figure 11-4). If the balance of loads within the boat were never to change, you could set the drive unit angle once and forget it. But loads do change in the real world. Say your plump Uncle Paul insists on riding ". . . in the front seat, where I can see everything." You'll need to adjust the trim angle to compensate. Usually you can compensate quite well.

The balance of forces is such that the prop will try to run at its optimum angle (perpendicular) no matter what, and since the drive unit forms an effective lever between the prop and transom mount, it can exert a pretty strong force on the boat as a whole, changing the boat's trim angle extensively. Figures 11-5 and 11-6 are exaggerated slightly for emphasis. While some boats will not react quite so much to a change of drive trim, remember that the load on your engine(s) will be least and speed at a given throttle setting highest when trim is right.

When you trim the drive(s) in (Figure 11-5), the resulting forces tend to lift the stern and push the bow down. Since this is not the best running angle, you might wonder why on earth we'd want to trim a boat this way. Well, there are several reasons. Say, for example, you have a baitwell full of water and bait, a fish box full of fresh catch, and a few fishing buddies in the cockpit along with a huge cooler full of cold sodas. You'll need more stern lift just to stay on plane. Even with a normal load, most planing hulls can use a little help getting up on plane when you start out. Remember, in exiting the displacement mode, the natural tendency is for the stern to settle. Forcing the bow down by trimming the drive(s) in helps the boat plane faster. Indeed, some stern-heavy boats would never plane if you couldn't trim the bow down when you first hit the throttle.

Figure 11-4

main
thrust

PROPER TRIM   *The main thrust is parallel to the surface; the boat runs on her lines.*

Figure 11-5

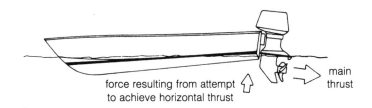

TRIMMED IN   *Trimming the drive unit(s) in (negative trim) adds stern lift. This can lead to "plowing" at cruise speeds, but it can also be helpful in getting a boat on plane more quickly.*

Trimming the drive(s) *out* (Figure 11-6) tends to lift the bow—which is just what you have to do when you have big old Uncle Paul up there in the bow seat. Of course it is possible to trim out too far. When you do, many planing hulls will begin to porpoise, bouncing across the water rather than gliding across it smoothly. When this happens, trim in slightly, and the boat should run at its best.

Figure 11-6

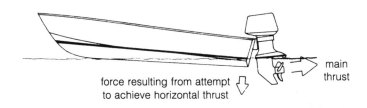

TRIMMED OUT   *Trimming the drive unit(s) out (positive trim) adds bow lift. A slight degree of positive trim is usually necessary for proper planing, but too much can cause porpoising. Positive trim is great for counteracting the effect of too much weight in the bow.*

The Trim Drill

Here's the basic procedure for achieving optimum trim underway. Trim the drive(s) all the way in before you start. Hit the throttle(s) and advance smoothly to wide open. When you get on plane, trim out until you reach maximum speed or until the boat begins to porpoise; then trim in slightly. Once you have the boat running at its best, throttle back to your intended cruising speed and fine-tune the trim to that speed. Strangely enough, it usually takes less time to make these moves than it does to describe them.

If you make a tight turn or slow down for any reason, you'll usually have to readjust the trim, tucking the drives slightly in to compensate for the drop in speed and changing attitude of the boat, then trimming out again when you regain your original speed. That's the advantage of power trim: You can fine-tune it as you need to.

One quick note on trim tabs. Planing hulls with transom power rarely need the added lift of trim tabs to get on plane, because tucking the drive(s) under will usually do the trick (though some particularly stern-heavy boats need all the help they can get). However, trim tabs are desirable on any planing boat to aid in lateral trim (when Uncle Paul insists on sitting on one side rather than up in the bow). Whether you use them all the time or only occasionally, you *will* use them. If the boat you're considering doesn't have them as standard equipment, be sure to include trim tabs among the extras.

What About Twins?

Some twin-propped transom-power systems offer counter-rotating props, thus eliminating torque-induced side thrust problems. When twin transom-power drives have the same rotation, torque problems can be multiplied, though proper adjustment of the trim fin on both units should reduce them to manageable proportions. Then there's the Volvo Duoprop we saw back in Chapter 6. It may not be the total answer, but in my limited experience with Duoprops, the absence of torque-induced side thrust is amazing, and the effect this has on boathandling is beautiful. I'll have more to say on specific twin transom power techniques in another chapter; for now I'll merely suggest that while some transom-powered boats with dual drives call for twin-screw handling techniques, most do not.

That pretty much covers the forces working on and within the boat itself, the ones we can adjust through manipulation of steering wheel, throttle, and, in the case of transom power, trim. Now it's time to move on to outside forces—ones we *can't* control, though we have to live with them just the same.

————————◆————————

12. The Influence of Wind

So far we have been dealing with the idyllic, hypothetical condition of no wind and no current. Were it only that way in real life, boathandling would be much easier. But of course we have to deal with nature, too. Wind and current exert their influence on our every move—often with tremendous impact. In this chapter, we'll take a look at wind alone, since it is the more influential.

Powerboats are usually affected by wind more than current because of their relatively shallow drafts and high superstructures. To appreciate this, you have only to look at boats on moorings in a tidal basin: Keel sailboats will inevitably swing with the tide, while powerboats will more often swing with the wind. For this reason, rather than snobbishness, harbormasters usually keep them segregated.

It might seem that we can do little but enjoy fair winds and suffer the foul. Actually, while the wind itself is beyond our control, how it *affects* us isn't. The overall effect depends on a number of factors, and it changes with the speed of the boat, the velocity of the wind (a 20-knot wind has four times the force of a 10-knot wind), and the direction from which the wind is blowing relative to the boat's heading. The accompanying diagrams show the effects of wind from different relative bearings.

Figure 12-1

MOORING MANNERS   *Generally speaking, moored powerboats swing with the wind, while keeled sailboats swing with the current. This truth is not always easy to prove, however, because for reasons quite unfathomable, there are always more sailboats than powerboats on moorings.*

In studying the illustrations, remember that another factor in the wind equation is the shape of the boat. Since every boat is different, experience will be the best teacher when it comes to learning how your boat behaves. I can, however, present some basics to build on.

A boat's shape, both above and below the waterline, is not merely a factor in the equation; it is a *huge* factor. Obviously, the more there is sticking up, particularly as compared with how much is sticking down, the more surface—"sail area," if you will—is available for the wind to act upon.

Since powerboats usually have less draft forward and less superstructure aft, wind most often has more influence on the bow. The exceptions are aft-cabin cruisers and motoryachts having considerable "house" all the way back. How wind affects such boats depends largely on the surface area of the superstructure relative to that of the underbody—if there's enough boat in the water, the large "sail area" in the stern may have little influence.

In Figure 12-2, we see the effects of wind on a boat that is making headway. We'll look first at what happens with a right-handed single-screw conventional drive and then consider how different power options alter the response.

Boat A has the wind dead ahead. This will slow the boat somewhat and magnify steering action, the latter response being the result of two factors: 1) Screw current will likely be greater for a given boat speed because of the added throttle you'll use to overcome the wind. 2) With every slight turn away from your initial heading straight into the wind, the bow gets an added push from the wind.

Figure 12-2

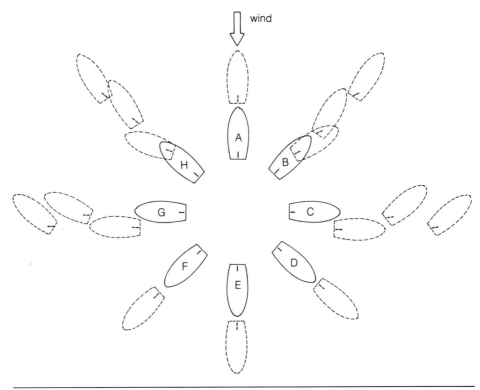

THE EFFECTS OF WIND ON A BOAT GOING AHEAD

Wind on the port bow (Boat B) tends to push the bow to starboard. Usually, a little left rudder is all you need to counter the wind and keep the boat on track. If the wind is slight and the boat has a natural tendency to veer to port, you may find that you can run straight with the rudder amidships.

The effect of wind abeam from the port side (C) depends on the superstructure. As mentioned above, however, most boats will see more push against the bow. A beam wind from the port side will move the boat to the right of its intended track and will require an answering left rudder.

Wind on the port quarter (D) generally has little effect other than to add to the natural tendency of a right-handed single-screw boat to veer to port.

A wind dead astern (E) probably has the least effect on steering, although at higher velocities it can create steering problems indirectly by putting you in following seas, which tend to kick the stern around. Its main influence is to increase your speed over the ground.

Wind on the starboard quarter (F) has little effect unless of great velocity.

Wind on the starboard beam (G) is similar to wind on the port beam with the added effect of increasing any tendency to veer to port; the same is true of wind on the starboard bow (H). In either case, answering with slight right rudder should hold you on your intended track.

Except for those instances in which wind exaggerates the tendency of a right-handed single-screw boat to veer to port, the wind's effect on twin-screw and transom-powered boats that are making headway will conform to the single-screw examples; relative above- and below-water "sail areas" and their fore-and-aft distributions are more important than drive systems.

Things change, however, for a boat moving astern (Figure 12-3). Most boats, most of the time, exhibit what is commonly called the weathervane effect. Simply

Figure 12-3

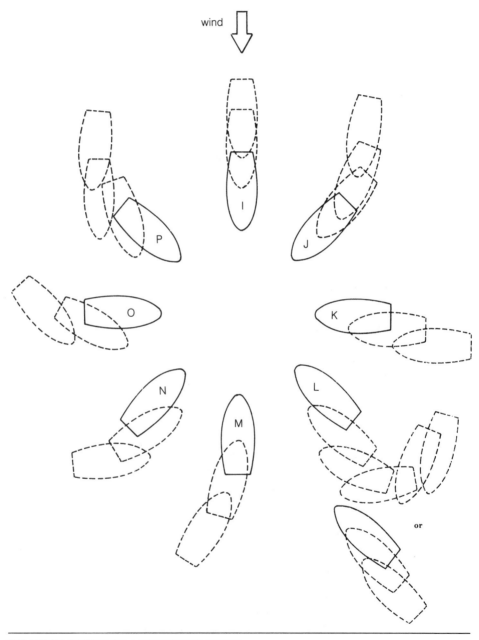

THE EFFECTS OF WIND ON A BOAT GOING ASTERN

stated, boats generally like to *back straight into the wind*. A drifting boat will often swing around until its stern faces the wind, and the application of power astern usually does little to change this attitude. For this reason, most boats will back directly into the wind (Boat I) even if their no-wind behavior displays a marked swing to port. Indeed, even boats having such strong single-screw side thrust behavior that they will back only to port in the absence of wind will often back to starboard if the wind is on the starboard quarter (J).

With wind on the starboard beam (K), you can probably back straight, though with a considerable side-set to port. You can also probably back to starboard, as you can when the wind is on the starboard bow (L), simply by letting the bow fall off the wind. In the latter case you can probably back straight—again with considerable side-set.

So far we have seen that as long as the wind is astern or at least over the starboard side, we can use it to overcome a right-handed single-screw boat's tendency to back to port. If the wind comes from ahead or over the port side, however, it reinforces the boat's normal swing to port. Regardless of rudder angle, the stern swing resulting from side thrust usually combines with the wind action on the bow to cause the boat to fall more and more off the wind. This means that the apparent wind will move gradually around from dead ahead (M) to the port bow (N) to the port beam (O) to the port quarter (P) and finally to dead astern.

Because we are dealing with a balance of forces, the wind velocity required to overcome side thrust in boats I, J, K, and L will depend on the force of the side thrust, the boat, and the throttle setting. You'll have to learn about your own boat on the water—unfortunately there are no shortcuts.

In the absence of strong side thrust—as on boats with counter-rotating twin screws or properly trimmed transom power—the behavior exhibited by boats M, N, and O will be absent. The behavior of boats P, I, and J, however, is not exclusive to single-screw drives. The weathervane effect is nearly universal. No matter how your boat is powered, most of the time it will be easiest to back straight into the wind, and whenever the wind is nearly dead astern, backing any other way but straight into it will be tough.

While wind is usually the predominant force of nature affecting powerboats, it is by no means the only one. In the next chapter we'll see what current does. And since neither wind nor current works alone, we'll also take a look at how they interact.

———————◆———————

13. What Current Does

As wind does, current can complicate maneuvers by pushing you off your intended track. As with wind, the manner in which current affects your boat depends on its strength and on how your boat reacts to it. Current *can* be a big factor in your boat's behavior in any situation, but because powerboats generally present less surface area to the water than to the wind, wind is often the bigger factor. So, at times, we can forget about current. But always? *No!*

If the current is strong enough and the wind gentle enough, current becomes the dominant force even with a boat of very shallow draft. This is particularly evident in rivers and in areas of strong tidal current. Thus, we must consider current along with wind in the operating equation, though here we can't be quite as broad in our approach to the problem. No little diagrams here!

Yet there are generalities to consider, and though each boat's reactions to current must ultimately be learned by experience, the learning will be easier if you have a knowledge of the generalities beforehand.

Draft and Speed

The current's effect on a boat is directly related to surface area of the underbody, yet draft is not the only consideration. The boat's speed through the water is also important, particularly so for a planing boat, whose draft decreases with an increase in speed.

The faster you go (even in a slow displacement boat, where "fast" is definitely a relative term), the less effect current will have as its speed becomes proportionately smaller. The other side of this coin is that in close-quarters maneuvers, every boat is in a displacement mode and going slowly (or should be!) so that the effect of current, if any, will be at its greatest just when it can upset you the most.

Pressure Points

Just as wind usually has its greatest effect on the bow because the boat's draft is less there, current usually does most of its work on the stern, where draft is greatest. In fact, in the absence of wind, there is a similar though opposite weathervane effect in which the bow swings to face the current. The operative phrase here is "in the absence of wind," something we rarely see.

A current from directly ahead will retard your progress and lower your speed over the ground for any given speed through the water. Likewise, a current from directly astern will move you ahead faster than your speed through the water would indicate. Currents from abeam will push you off your intended course, currents at 45 degrees on either bow will push you off course and retard progress, and similar currents from astern will advance you as they move you off course. Yet we can't put these elementary generalities into diagrams as we did with wind because current will take a backseat to wind in many situations, and its total effect is usually a result of its interaction with the wind.

When wind and current move in the same direction, their forces are additive. That is, a 15-knot wind and a 5-knot current from the same direction will act upon your boat like a 20-knot wind from that direction. When wind opposes current, however, the net result is rarely a direct subtraction: A 5-knot current opposing a 15-knot wind will *not* reduce the wind's influence to that of a 10-knot blow. Rather, the wind's effect will be slightly diminished but still dominant. If the current is stronger than the wind—for example, a 5-knot current and a 3-knot wind—the current may dominate, though the ultimate interaction depends on your boat.

When wind and current are neither in opposition nor in the same direction, the net effect depends on their relative strengths and your boat's particular behavior, which is difficult if not impossible to predict. In the next chapter, however, I'll offer some advice on how to learn quickly under the circumstances of the moment.

Because current usually has a stronger effect on the stern and thus your boat *can* tend to swing into it, single-screw boats (and low-powered vessels of any configuration) are usually most maneuverable when the bow is headed into the current. With twin screws, however, your control forces are in the stern and you have more options as to how those forces work for you. For this reason, especially if wind and current are working together, you can often maintain the best control of a twin-screw boat by backing it into the current. A slight increase or decrease in engine speed can pull you faster or slower astern as conditions demand; alternating clutches in and out of gear will let you steer.

———◆———

PART

THREE

THE HOWS OF
POWERBOAT
HANDLING

14. Know Your Boat

Learning exactly how your boat behaves in every situation is or ought to be a never-ending process. The learning is rarely a chore, and it is deeply satisfying to know intimately a particular boat's every nuance of behavior. Long before that day is reached, however, you need at least a general idea of what will happen under given circumstances. Indeed, you should have this knowledge before you attempt your first close-quarters maneuver in an unfamiliar boat.

Because I do a lot of deliveries and boat tests, I spend a great deal of time aboard boats that are new to me. I've had to develop a drill to introduce me to a boat's responses, and I'd like to share it here. Naturally, the drill varies with the type of boat, and I'll cover each in due time. With any boat, however, it is best to approximate initially (as closely as you can in the real world) the "no-wind, no-current, boat-behavior-only" situation covered in Chapters 9, 10, and 11. Look for an area with little current, adequate shelter from the prevailing wind, sufficient depth, and ample maneuvering room. And though you are looking for a fairly unrestricted open area, look also for landmarks to help you gauge direction and distance. This testing ground may sound difficult to find, but every boating area I've ever known has several such places nearby.

Single Screw

Let's begin our real world approach as we did the theoretical: with single-screw conventional drive. First, you want to learn how big a problem side thrust will be. Since side thrust is greater when going astern, we'll check it out first. With the boat dead in the water, set the rudder amidship. (If there's no rudder angle indicator, and with most pleasureboats there won't be, count the number of turns of the steering wheel from hard over right to hard over left and then come back half the total.) Put the clutch in reverse and increase the throttle. You'll be able to see how much the stern swings and how steerable the boat is. You'll see how much sternway is required for the rudder action to overtake side thrust (if, indeed, it will—some single-screw boats cannot be steered when backing, no matter what!) and you will learn whether you have a right-handed or left-handed wheel. The stern will swing to port with a right-handed wheel, to starboard with a left.

With the rudder back amidship, put the clutch in forward gear and ease the throttle up to cruising speed. Using landmarks, see how much you veer to port (with a right-handed wheel) and how much right rudder it takes to go straight. Then come back to idle speed, and use reverse to stop. How far do you advance before stopping, and how much stern swing do you get in the process? You should also see how long it takes the boat to come to a stop without applying reverse, and how much rudder action you have in the absence of screw current.

Next, try going ahead again at cruising speed and observing the differences between port and starboard turns and between stern swing and bow swing. In short, you want to determine how closely your boat's behavior matches the typical single-screw behavior outlined in Chapter 9.

Twin Screws

Twin screws give you a few other things to test. For example, in stopping with both screws astern, you shouldn't see any stern swing, but it's still a good idea to find out how much effect momentum has—how long it takes to come to a stop from various speeds ahead with varying degrees of reverse throttle.

You also need to find out how much rudder action you get at maneuvering speeds both ahead and astern—and be sure to check the difference in rudder action with and without screw current (engines in or out of gear). This determines how much attention you should pay to rudder angle when you are executing a maneuver or, put another way, how much help you'll get from changing the rudder angle. As I pointed out back in Chapter 9, the effectiveness of a rudder is primarily dependent on the screw current across it. Because rudders are often located such that screw current is a lesser factor than side thrust until the throttles are advanced considerably, side thrust is often far more influential on boat behavior than rudder angle—especially in negotiating typical twin-screw maneuvers.

Try putting the rudders amidship and splitting the clutches; that is, put one ahead, the other astern. The boat should start to spin around. Now turn the steering wheel in the direction you are spinning. If you have put the port gear in forward and the starboard gear astern, turn the wheel for full right rudder. Look for a change in the radius of your turning circle. If the turn gets considerably tighter with an increase in rudder angle, the rudders are helping a lot. If they make little or no difference, you may be able to forget them in many maneuvering situations.

Now bring the clutches to neutral and wait for the boat to stop spinning. When it has settled down, leave the steering wheel at full right rudder and split the clutches the opposite way—starboard ahead, port astern. If you didn't see much effect from the rudders before, you won't now; the boat will start to spin the other way. But if the rudders aided the turn before, the boat will now slide to port instead of spinning. If you see even the slightest indication of this, try playing the throttles to see whether running one engine or the other a little faster makes a difference. Then try taking each engine alternately in and out of gear (but don't disengage the clutch of an engine you have revved up until you first bring the throttle back to idle). You'll get a good indication of whether this boat can be walked sideways or not, how difficult a process it is, and what you have to do to make it happen, all of which can be extremely valuable information.

In Chapter 6 I suggested that twin screws do not automatically provide get-home power when one engine fails because some twin-screw boats simply won't operate properly on a single screw. Now is the time to find out whether this boat will.

Put the rudders amidship, then put one engine in gear and advance its throttle. Initially, you'll probably see a turn toward the opposite side. That is, if you've put the starboard engine in gear, you will see a turn to port. If the boat is operable on one engine, however, it will begin to straighten out, and at some point you should be able to steer the boat—even to starboard. If the boat just keeps turning to port, forget running on one engine.

Even if you observe near total control when going forward, you should still find out what happens going astern. Remember the single-screw tendency to back only one way, and consider the implications of moving that screw off the centerline. Even if they behave well on one engine when going ahead, most twin-screw boats show exaggerated single-screw behavior when forced to *back* on one. It's better to find out before you need to know.

Transom Power

If you have an outboard or sterndrive boat, the first thing you want to find out is what happens when you change trim—how much you must trim in to get on plane, and how much you can trim out before the boat begins to porpoise.

Next, you need to try some low-speed maneuvers to determine how sensitive the steering is at idle speed and how much steering ability remains when you take the engine(s) out of gear.

Though backing a transom-powered boat is generally easier than backing a single-screw inboard, you should still try going astern to see exactly how steerable this boat is in reverse. You should also determine how much side thrust remains (remember, transom power can reduce but not necessarily eliminate it) and thus how much initial stern swing you get when you put the engine(s) in reverse. This knowledge can come in handy when you begin docking practice. Since the angle at which the prop attacks the water is one of the factors influencing side thrust, be sure to assess the changes that occur as you change trim at maneuvering speed.

If you have twins, are the props counter-rotating? Look at the propeller blades. If both blades are pitched in the same direction, they must rotate in the same direction. If they are opposite, you have counter-rotation. (Since manufacturers are rather proud of counter-rotating props, the units will probably say so—boldly, I might add—somewhere in the specifications.)

You don't *need* to know whether you have counter-rotating props, but the knowledge will help explain the behavior you are about to evaluate. Lacking them, the odds are you will not see typical twin-screw behavior with twin transom power. However, the spacing between the drives can sometimes be as much (or more) of a factor.

You need to determine whether you have twin-screw action or merely single screw doubled up. Put the "rudders" (drives) amidship and split the clutches. See how tight a circle you turn. Then put the rudders hard over one way or the other and put only the outside engine (starboard, for a left-hand turn) ahead, leaving the other in neutral. If the twin-screw action gave you a tighter turn, use it—you have the capability. If the rudder-action turn was tighter, forget that you have twins when it comes to maneuvering. We won't try mixing clutch and rudder action as we did with twin inboards, because with transom power the thrust of the reversed engine is fully directed, unlike the screw current from a reversed inboard, which doesn't flow over the rudder. This means that trying to split the clutches and use the steering wheel at the same time usually will result in a looser turn than you get just from splitting the clutches. For similar reasons, it is rarely possible to walk a twin-screw transom-powered boat sideways. Thanks to greater maneuverability in general, however, it's no great loss.

Adding Nature

Since we have done the above exercises in a location that's as free from nature's influences as we could possibly find, it's now time to move. Seek out wind and current and do the drill all over from the top, observing the changes nature adds as you go along. If you move around to different locations, you can find quite a variety of combinations. Time alone will offer you the rest. You'll get an *infinite* variety if you stay with it long enough.

———————◆———————

15. Boathandling in Wind and Current

In the following chapters, you'll see a "by-the-numbers" approach to typical boathandling situations. The caveat is that boathandling can't be done strictly by the numbers; every experience is unique. Each time you make a landing or set your anchor or do any of the myriad maneuvers I'm about to outline, you'll be doing it for the first time *under that particular set of conditions*. Wind varies in both velocity and direction, as does current, and their interaction varies further by the relative strengths and directions of the component forces and their respective influences on your boat. Add the changing load and trim conditions aboard your vessel, and you are faced with an infinite set of variables.

In any boathandling situation you have to modify the basic procedures (which hold true in principle for all situations) to suit the specific conditions you face at the time. While this may sound ominous, in actual practice it isn't difficult at all. The main thing you have to remember is: *Don't try to fight Mother Nature!*

Let me put it another way. In past chapters we have seen that, left to its own devices, there are certain things your boat will do by itself. Wind and current will do other things to it. If you plan your maneuvers to work with these tendencies, boathandling will be simpler than if you fight them. In truth, if you fight them, you may win sometimes, but most often you won't. In the long run, it's not only smarter but much, much easier to get nature to work with you, and that means working with nature.

Gauging Wind and Current

First, you need to determine, to the best of your ability, what wind and current are doing. Your eyes are an excellent tool. To gauge the wind, look at flags and pennants on other boats or ashore. If you are about to make a landing, you care less whether the wind is from the north, south, or some other point of the compass than whether it is blowing onto, away from, or parallel to the pier, or from points in between. You also need to know, in simple terms, how hard it is blowing, and thus whether it will be a major or minor influence. Are the flags really

Figure 15-1

READING THE WIND *A flag waving in the breeze is a perfect clue as to which way the wind is blowing. In this situation you'd use a "wind off the pier" approach.*

flapping, barely moving, or hanging limp? Lacking flags, look for smoke, trees, even birds, which usually sit facing the wind.

You can gauge current similarly, though the signs are not always as numerous nor as obvious. Tethered floating objects such as buoys usually give you a hint. Whether they are aids to navigation, mooring devices, or the visible markers of crustacean corrals doesn't matter at all. Anchored boats can help, too; just remember that most powerboats will swing with the wind—look at deep-draft vessels such as keeled sailboats for signs of current. Even fixed objects such as pilings or bridge piers and fender systems will show telltale signs of current in the ripples that form on both the up- and downstream sides. The stronger the current (i.e., the more trouble it can give you), the more visible the signs. If you can't see its signs (providing there are objects there to help you), you probably don't have to worry about current.

Looking for these signs takes conscious effort initially, but with a little practice you'll find yourself processing clues constantly without a bit of thought.

It doesn't matter whether the predominant force is wind or current, since it is inevitably the interaction of forces that produces the observed effect on your boat. The good news is that determining the combined effect of outside forces is easy. You need only bring the throttle(s) back to idle, take the clutch or clutches out of gear, and wait until the boat settles dead in the water. Then wait a few seconds more, and you'll see—or more important, feel—the effect. Is the boat

Figure 15-2

READING THE CURRENT *Look closely at the ripples around the piling and you can quickly tell which way the current is flowing—and often, how strong it is.*

still sliding forward? Have you begun to move backward? Sideways? Are you swinging? How fast and which way? To plan your maneuver, you need only factor in these natural movements with your boat's known behavior under power, and you can fairly well predict the ultimate behavior and make your moves accordingly.

To learn more about your boat's behavior under the conditions of the moment, make a dry run in open water before you try the real thing in tight quarters. If you miscalculate the first time, try again. Some dockside wiseguys may wonder why you stay out there fooling around, but taking time to fully appreciate the conditions of the moment can help you avoid the day when they wonder why you hit the pier so hard.

Even after you've become adept enough to skip the dry runs, you can benefit from taking a moment to check out wind and current before you commit to a maneuver. I still do.

16· Docking a Single-Screw Inboard

Before tackling this chapter you might read Chapters 9 through 15, if you have not already done so. It will make the explanation of docking more meaningful and a lot easier to follow.

Note that in the following explanations I often use the word "wind" to simplify things. Please read it to mean the combined force of wind and current.

Docking can be a traumatic experience. Usually the last event of the day, your return to the marina can set the tone for your memories of the entire outing. When the landing goes well, you may breathe a sigh of relief. When it doesn't, you may curse. Either way, you're usually glad when it's over because chances are you're tired and ready to head home. Your crew is probably even more tired and less help than you'd hope for, so you're left somewhat to your own devices. To make matters worse, there's usually a crowd watching to see how well you do (and offering plenty of free, though conflicting, advice). That's the stuff trauma is built of. I can't guarantee perfect landings, but if you have an idea what to do before you actually have to do it, you should be able to take some of the hard knocks out of the process. Look at the diagrams, think about the process involved, temper the approach each time as suggested in Chapter 15, and you should be OK.

Single-Screw Stern Swing

Exaggerated stern swing in reverse, the action which can so often be a curse, can be a blessing when bringing a boat alongside a float or pier. If you approach the landing with the side to which the stern will swing when you reverse the engine—port side for a right-handed screw, starboard for a left—the swing you can't avoid will bring the stern in smartly as you come to a stop.

Let's take it by the numbers. Look at Figure 16-1. In this illustration we're assuming a right-handed wheel, so we're coming into land port side to. The initial approach (1) should be at an angle of 20 degrees or so, the exact angle being determined by the force and direction of wind and current, as we'll discuss in a moment. When you get closer to the dock (2), ease the throttle to minimum steerageway and make final adjustments in your approach angle to allow for wind and current. As you near the pier (3), put the clutch in neutral and give full right rudder. This will start bringing the boat parallel to the pier. Finally, as your bow *almost* touches, put the clutch astern and apply just enough throttle to stop the boat and swing the stern in (4).

Now let's introduce some wind (again, read this as the net effect of wind and current). If it is behind you (thus pushing you forward), throttle back sooner and (probably) apply reverse sooner than you would in an absence of wind. If the wind is from ahead, you need to stay under power longer to get to your desired berth, since the wind will be pushing you back. It is usually easier to land heading into the wind and current.

If the wind is pushing you toward or away from the pier, you must modify the approach angle and your rudder action to account for it. Let's check it out.

Figure 16-1

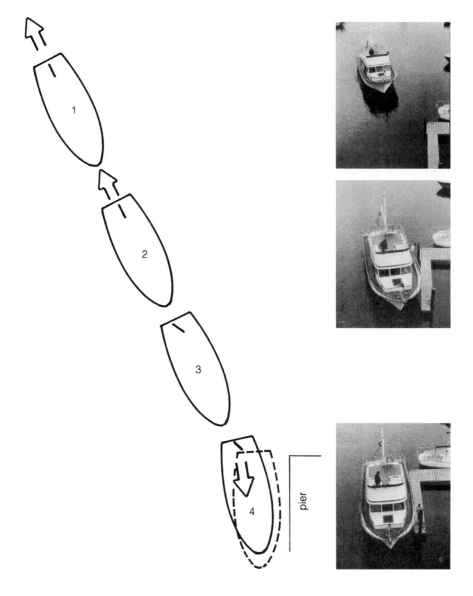

DOCKING A SINGLE-SCREW INBOARD: THE BASIC APPROACH   *Arrows indicate direction of thrust. For clarity, only the main thrust is shown.*

Wind Blowing On the Pier

A wind pushing you toward the pier presents at once the easiest and perhaps the most difficult landing situation. It's the easiest because you'll end up against the pier even if you do nothing! It's difficult because your object is to make *gentle* landings, and with nature forcing you against the pier, it is not so easy to land softly.

Figure 16-2 shows a wind-on situation. The secret is to come in at a flatter angle and to start the approach farther away. It may help to imagine that you are landing at a pier that is closer to you than the real one, since you will probably move toward the actual pier faster than you'd prefer.

Note that in this case you'll probably have to use slight right rudder to keep the bow out. Here's another tip to help soften the landing: Instead of continuing to slide in sideways—as you'll be doing through much of the approach—let the bow come in when you get close, and then roll onto the pier on the curve of the bow. This rolling action will usually be softer than hitting flat. Use a fender or two to soften the landing even more.

If the wind is really strong, you may want to take yet another approach. In Figure 16-3, we come in with the wind dead astern. Remember the weathervane effect? Let it work for you. By applying power astern, you can counter the force of the wind, and the weathervane effect will keep the stern from swinging. As you ease off on the throttle (2), the wind will push you in until you are close enough (about 1½ boat lengths off) to put the clutch in neutral and the rudder hard right (3), which will start you swinging parallel to the pier. When you are nearly in place (4), another short application of power astern should be enough to stop you and complete the procedure. Since the wind will aid in making the stern swing in, it's best to emphasize "short." Too much power astern will most likely result in a bump and bang.

Figure 16-2

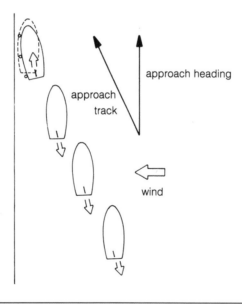

approach heading

approach track

wind

DOCKING A SINGLE-SCREW INBOARD—WIND BLOWING ONTO THE PIER

THE HOWS OF POWERBOAT HANDLING

Figure 16-3

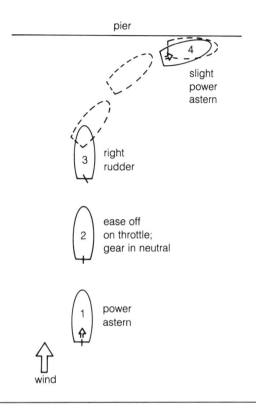

pier

4

slight
power
astern

3 right
rudder

2 ease off
on throttle;
gear in neutral

1 power
astern

wind

DOCKING A SINGLE-SCREW INBOARD: STRONG WIND ON PIER

Wind Blowing Off the Pier

When Mother Nature seems to be doing her best to keep you away from your intended landing spot, you may be tempted to curse her loudly. But in truth, you should be somewhat thankful, because, though it can sometimes be the most work, landing with the wind off the dock almost assures you of coming in gently.

The key here is a broader approach angle—say 30 degrees or perhaps more, depending on the wind (Figure 16-4). You'll probably need left rudder and a bit more throttle to keep the bow from being pushed away. When you are almost touching the pier, take the engine out of gear, give hard right rudder, and finally apply a short burst of power in reverse to stop your forward motion and bring the stern in. As I said, this should result in a very gentle landing. The nice part is that if you react too soon, the wind will merely take you out, and you can try again.

If the wind is very strong, your moment at dockside will be brief, so it is essential that you get a line ashore and made fast immediately. As we'll see in Chapter 20, you may even need that line to complete the maneuver.

Figure 16-4

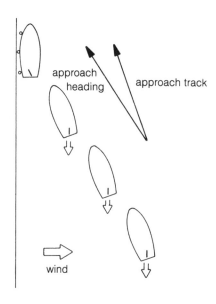

approach
heading

approach track

wind

DOCKING A SINGLE-SCREW INBOARD: WIND BLOWING OFF THE PIER

Against the Thrust

All other things being equal, the added help stern thrust can provide makes it worth landing "right side" to the pier (port for right-handed, starboard for left-handed screws). All other things are not always equal, however, and at times we have no choice but to land "wrong side" to. The problem then is that the last-minute burst of power astern swings us away from the pier as we stop, definitely not the desired action. We have to allow for it by getting the stern closer to the pier before we finish the maneuver. Figure 16-5 illustrates the routine. The initial approach is similar to landing port side to (again using a right-handed wheel). Set an approach angle of about 20 degrees (1), and ease off on the throttle as you get close (2). When you are nearly there, put the clutch in neutral and give left rudder (3). Then comes the big difference. Before you reach the stopping point, give an additional short burst of power forward to set the stern swinging to starboard (4). Then quickly come to neutral, put the clutch astern, and give a short burst of power to stop (5). If you set up just enough starboard stern swing from the burst of forward power to cancel the stern swing resulting from the application of power astern, you'll come to a stop just where you want to be. Too much forward power can swing the stern in too far too soon. Too little, and the stern will still swing away when you apply reverse. This move will improve with practice as you get to know just what it takes to achieve the desired balance with your boat.

Figure 16-5

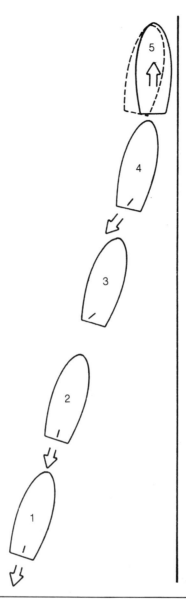

DOCKING A SINGLE-SCREW INBOARD: AGAINST THE THRUST

The downside of docking "wrong side" to is that most of the time you won't have to, so this maneuver gets less practice than others. Practice it once in a while just to keep your touch.

The upside is that most of the time you will have a choice. Though single-screw boats are not as maneuverable as boats with twin screws, you can often put yourself in a position to dock the desired way despite prevailing circumstances. In the next chapter, we'll find out how.

17. The "Impossible" Moves with a Single-Screw Boat

Without question, twin-screw boats are much more maneuverable than single-screw, particularly when it comes to backing or turning in tight quarters. Merely because these moves are easier for twins, however, doesn't mean we can't do them with singles. This chapter shows how to turn obstacles into advantages.

The following descriptions are for a right-handed screw. All the actions should be reversed for a left-handed screw.

And Back We Go!

As we have seen, when you apply power astern, side thrust tends to overcome sternway in degrees ranging from mere nuisance to major obstruction. Couple this with rather poor steering action astern (at best), and backing can be a real chore.

Chore though it may be, you *can* do it. A little right rudder (Figure 17-1) will sometimes suffice to counter stern swing and let you back straight (or nearly so). If your boat will behave this way, consider yourself lucky. Most will not. Be careful with the right rudder, and don't use too much because it is tough on the steering gear to back *against* a turned rudder.

If your boat is like most, it won't back straight and will veer to the left of your intended track. This calls for a little shuffle with your hands. Use one hand to turn the steering wheel quickly for hard left rudder and the other to go from reverse to forward. If you apply a short but strong burst of forward power, the stern will swing back to starboard without your losing much sternway in the process.

As the stern swings to the right of your intended course, put the rudder back to slightly right of amidship and again ease the power astern. You may have to repeat this procedure several times if you want to back very far. On the other hand, once you get the boat straightened out after its initial swing to port, you may find that the steering ability you gain as your speed astern increases will be enough to keep you going the way you want by rudder action alone. If you can steer in reverse after you gain sufficient sternway, you can also try kicking the stern to starboard *before* you begin backing up. Just be sure your boat will respond this way before you try it in close quarters.

How you finish the procedure depends on how steerable your boat is in reverse and which way you plan to go after you finish backing. If you plan to head to starboard, you can let the stern swing to port as soon as you clear the obstructions you are backing out of. If you plan to head to port, you'll need to back far enough to allow turning room.

Restricted Turning

Ah, turning room. If you have a single-screw boat, undoubtedly there will be many times you'll wish you could spin it in scarcely more than its own length—as

Figure 17-1

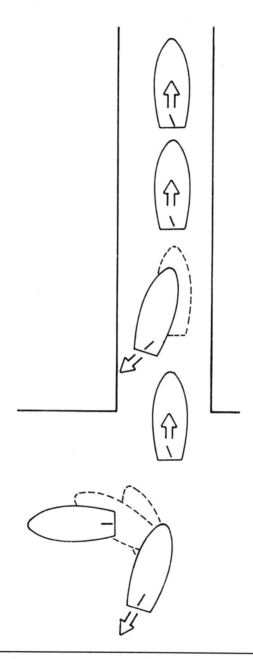

TAKING A SINGLE-SCREW BOAT STRAIGHT BACK *For clarity, only the main thrust is shown.*

the twin-screw skippers do. Well, you can't, and that's something you have to learn to live with. But you can come close. Again, use the boat's natural tendencies to help you out.

Figure 17-2

only main thrust is shown

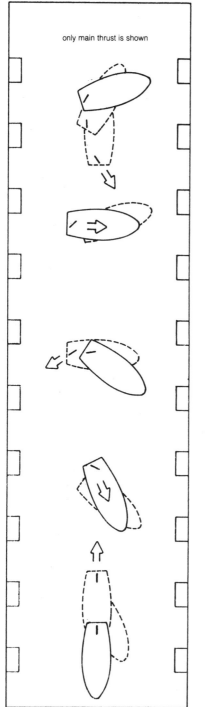

TURNING IN TIGHT QUARTERS (SINGLE-SCREW INBOARD)

The secret in this case is to couple the boat's inevitable stern swing in reverse with the stern swing you can create from short bursts of forward thrust with full rudder. If you have a right-handed screw, you can turn easily to starboard in little more than a boat length if you work the throttle and clutch properly. Short but strong bursts are the key.

Figure 17-2 shows what happens. With the clutch in neutral, put the rudder over hard right. Then give a strong, short burst of forward power. Before the boat can advance very far, it will start to swing to starboard. If you were to leave it in forward, you would begin to see some advance. But you don't. Instead, you quickly bring the throttle back to idle, shift the clutch to neutral, pause a brief moment, then put the clutch astern and give another burst of power. The initial stern swing you get from the side thrust astern coupled with the swing you started with the burst of power ahead will continue the spin without causing any sternway. Then, before sternway has the chance to develop, another shift through neutral into forward and a short burst of power will add yet more swing. Again, if you were to allow the forward thrust to take over, you would begin to straighten out and see some forward motion. But since you apply the power in a burst and then again shift to apply power in a short burst astern, you will see yet more stern swing without movement either forward or astern.

Repeat the procedure one or two more times, and you'll be turned around. Remember, you have to keep the power bursts short so as to accentuate stern swing without producing headway or sternway. Leave the engine in gear too long in either direction, and you'll defeat your purpose. If you make the bursts short but strong, you can *almost* duplicate a twin-screw pirouette.

----------◆----------

18. Docking a Twin-Screw Inboard

Wait a minute! Just because you have a twin-screw boat doesn't mean that the details of single-screw handling aren't important to you. They are. If you are jumping in here to get what you need to know without wasting time on the unnecessary, please go back and read those chapters first. It will help.

The Twin-Screw Approach

One of the reasons for reading the chapter on docking a single-screw boat is that when coming alongside a float or pier, you do essentially the same things with a twin screw that you do with a single. For example, the suggestions regarding the changes you should make in your angle of approach to allow for nature apply equally to singles and twins, so I'm not going to repeat them. The main differ-ence is that you no longer have a "right side" and "wrong side" for easy landings. With twin screws, you can put either side to the pier with equal ease. And that can be a huge advantage.

Rudders versus Clutches

Another difference is that you can ignore the rudders and maneuver the twin-screw boat with clutches and throttles alone. Whether you use the rudders or leave them amidship depends greatly on how much rudder action you get when the engines are out of gear or at idle. If rudders are a significant factor in handling your boat, by all means use them—every little bit helps. But if you have found that rudder angle makes little difference at maneuvering speeds (see Chapters 10 and 14) why go to the trouble of messing with the steering wheel in addition to the clutches and throttles?

We might as well recognize the truth that the first time you face the console of a twin-screw boat you can't help but wonder how you are going to do it all with just two hands. Even with single-lever control (clutch and throttle in the same handle), you seem to need one hand for each engine and another for steering. If the throttle and clutch levers are separate, the thought of handling twin screws can be even more intimidating! But it needn't be. Fortunately, two hands are plenty, even when you have two throttles and two clutches (though single-lever controls are much easier to use and a nice plus).

The Docking Drill

Let's come alongside a float. Since we did most of our single-screw landings port side to, let's come in starboard side to this time, simply because *we can*. In fact, let's do it twice, once without rudders and once with, just to see the differences.

In Figure 18-2 we see a typical landing. As with the single screw, approach angle is about 20 degrees off the face of the pier. (Remember, you have to adjust this angle to accommodate wind and current, just as with the single screw.) Since you are steering only with the engines, it may be necessary to take one or the other out of gear to swing the bow slightly. At position 2, let's say you're being pushed onto the dock faster than you'd like. Simply take the outboard engine (the one *away* from the pier—in this case the port) out of gear, and the bow will swing slightly away. When you get close to your desired dock space (3), take the other engine out of gear and coast toward the pier. When the bow is about to touch (4), put the outboard engine astern to reduce headway and swing the stern in. Since a twin-screw prop in reverse is essentially an exaggerated single screw—a result of its being off center—sometimes the stern will swing too much when you use the outboard engine alone. In this case, put the other engine astern also (5) to cancel the swing. If putting both engines astern should go beyond stopping and begin to produce sternway, you can cancel it with a quick application of forward on both engines and still remain parallel to the pier.

For the sake of brevity, I just simplified the steering actions involved at position 2. In the real world, you might have to put the engine back in gear if the bow swings out farther than you want, and you may have to take the starboard engine out of gear to help swing it back. You might even have to repeat these actions a few times to keep the boat going the way you want. This is one of those maneuvers that can only be described in broad terms, since every boat and situation will be different. Just remember that if you are steering with the engines, it may take several shifts of either or *both* clutches to fine-tune your final approach.

Figure 18-1

Figure 18-2

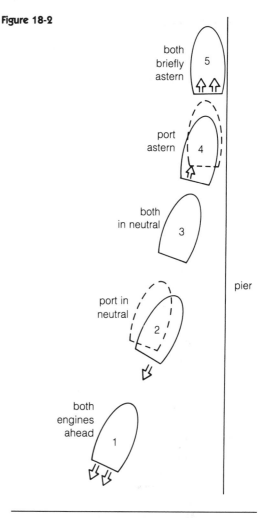

both
briefly
astern
5

port
astern
4

both
in neutral
3

port in
neutral
2

pier

both
engines
ahead
1

TWIN-SCREW DOCKING: THE BASICS   *For clarity, only the main thrust (arrows) is shown.*

HOW MANY HANDS DO YOU NEED?   *When twin-screw boats have dual-lever controls (two throttles, two clutches), the console can be intimidating. After all, you only have two hands. But that's all you need. Single-lever controls do make it easier, but you can manage quite nicely without them.*

With the Rudders' Help

The technique I just described will work with any twin-screw inboard boat. You can use it without reservation even if you are unsure whether the boat responds well to its rudder at maneuvering speeds. "So," you may wonder, "why bother to do it any other way?" The answer is that if your boat *will* respond to its rudders, the variety of movements you can get from different combinations of clutch, throttle, and rudders makes the extra effort well worth it.

Let's try the same landing again, this time adding rudder action. Figure 18-3 shows the basic approach—roughly 20 degrees off the pier. Turn the steering wheel at (2) to fine-tune the approach angle for ambient wind and current. When

Figure 18-3

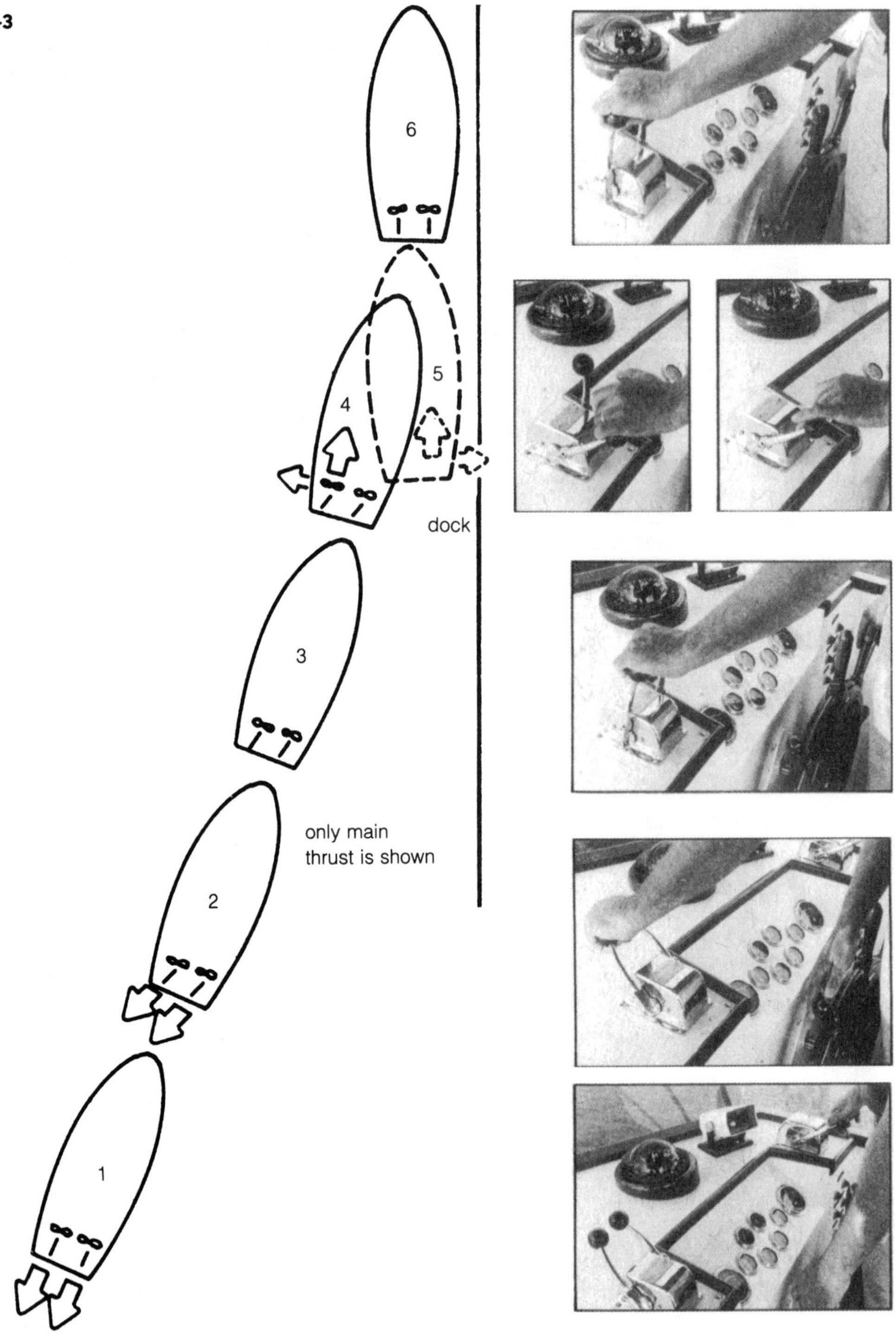

6

5

4

dock

3

only main
thrust is shown

2

1

TWIN SCREW DOCKING: ADDING RUDDER ACTION

you get close to your desired dock space (3), take the engines out of gear and coast toward the pier, applying left rudder to begin swinging the stern. Here's the exciting part. If the boat will slide sideways (see Chapter 14), you can essentially parallel park by using a lot of left rudder with the port clutch in forward (4) and perhaps the starboard astern. When you're just about in place, straighten the rudders and take both engines out of gear (5).

Using the rudders to steer frees the throttles and clutches to control speed. If leaving both engines in gear causes an overly rapid approach even at idle speed, you can take one engine out of gear to cut your thrust in half and keep the boat pointed in the right direction with adjustments to rudder angle. Because side thrust can be a potent factor even when you apply rudder action, you may have to alternate engines to keep precise directional control. That is, rudder action might not be enough to keep the thrust of a single engine from swinging the stern (and thus the opposite bow) more than you'd like.

Even if your boat won't "slide" sideways, you may be able to walk her in sideways with left rudder by putting the port engine alternately ahead and astern (Figure 18-4), thus swinging first the bow and then the stern closer to the pier. In this case, most likely you won't need to do anything with the starboard engine until you are almost at the float or pier, at which point putting it ahead will stop the bow from swinging in too much, and putting it astern will do the same thing for the other end.

Figure 18-4

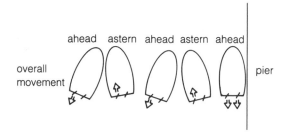

"WALKING" SIDEWAYS WITH TWINS   *Swing exaggerated for emphasis.*

Once again a reminder: We landed starboard side to in this illustration to contrast it with the one-sided approach preferred with a single screw. You could come in port side to just as easily simply by swapping the starboard and port actions described above.

Backing

As we've seen in previous chapters, a major advantage of twin-screw power is better handling when going astern. This makes it much easier to back your boat into a slip, as is preferred by many dockmasters and virtually required for sportfishermen.

Figure 18-5

BACKING IN *Because sportfishermen are easy to maneuver, and because having the cockpit next to the pier makes it easier to unload the catch, sportfishing skippers almost always back into their slips.*

Docking stern to is common in Europe, so common it's called a Mediterranean moor. In North America it is usual to simplify matters by sinking outer pilings off the ends of the slips and inserting finger piers between slips. Let's see how to use twin screws for a typical American-style stern-to docking maneuver.

The maneuver itself is easy in its basic form. As Figure 18-6 shows, it's a matter of splitting the clutches to initiate the turn (2), then putting both astern to back in (3), and finally both forward long enough to stop (4).

The variations (or complications, if you wish) are introduced because, despite the superior maneuverability of a twin-screw boat, you have to take nature into consideration, or the move won't go as smoothly as you'd like.

Effects of Wind

In Figure 18-7 three boats are backing into their respective slips. Boat A, having the wind on its stern, will initiate its turn before arriving at its slip because the wind will keep moving it as it turns. Since wind usually works more on the bow, the bow should point slightly into the wind before backing (2). The wind will then help straighten it out.

Boat B, approaching into the wind, will run beyond its slip and begin backing sooner because, again, the wind will help swing the bow.

The skipper of boat C didn't allow for the wind and is in an awkward position because of it.

Figure 18-6

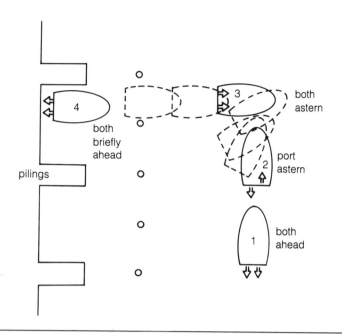

BACKING IN: THE TECHNIQUE

Effects of Current

Because current works more on the stern, it is often easier to maneuver with the current behind you. In Figure 18-8, boat A proceeds just as he would with the wind behind—with one important exception. If current is the major force, you don't need to swing as far around before backing. In fact, with a strong current behind you, you should begin backing *before* you are lined up with the slip, because your stern will continue to swing downcurrent as you back.

A boat approaching into the current, as is boat B, will be better off turning completely around before getting to the slip and executing the final portions of the maneuver going astern. Here it's usually advisable to back slightly beyond the slip so that when the current sets you down, you'll be in the right position.

Again, failure to allow for nature has put boat C in difficulty.

You've probably noticed that we didn't bother with the rudders this time. That's because, as I mentioned above, twin-screw maneuvers can always be done without them. If rudder action is a big factor on your boat, you can use the steering wheel to help counter the forces of nature. In the above examples, for instance, slight right rudder might have helped slow the bow swing when wind was the major force, and slight left rudder might help keep the stern into the current as you back up. However, this depends greatly on your boat's responses and your ability to find the rudder angle that will help the most. These factors take time to learn, and you will probably find it much easier initially to ignore your rudders.

Figure 18-7

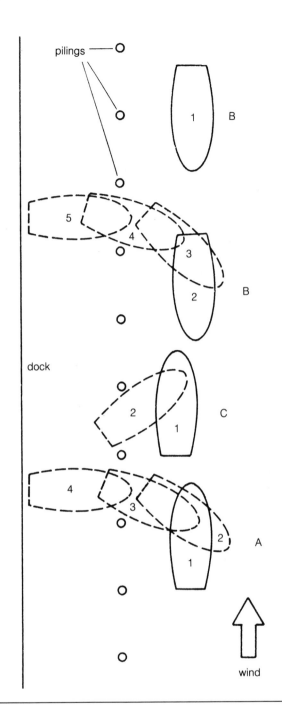

ALLOWING FOR WIND

Figure 18-8

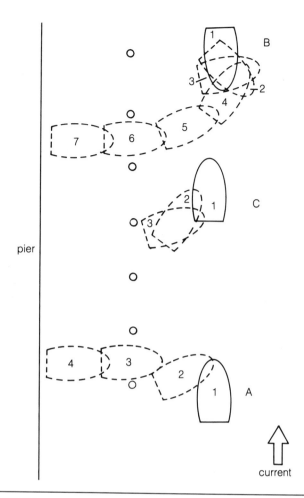

ALLOWING FOR CURRENT

19. Docking Transom-Powered Boats

Transom-powered boats, whether outboard or sterndrive, don't handle quite the same as inboards, for reasons examined in Chapter 11. Yet our objectives remain the same when putting a boat into its berth at a pier, which means that many of the suggestions made previously still apply. Indeed, the handling of transom-powered boats is most easily described in terms of differences and similarities relative to conventional drives.

Side Thrust

We've already covered this, but it's so important that I feel compelled to bring it up again: One of the big differences between conventional drives and transom power (perhaps the *major* one) is that outboards and sterndrives can often drastically reduce, if not eliminate completely, the side thrust of inboard-drive systems. Whether this is a blessing or a curse depends on your point of view and the situation at hand. It surely is nice to see the stern of a conventional inboard swing neatly into place alongside the pier when you apply reverse power to stop forward motion. On the other hand, not being able to back a single-screw inboard the way you might desire is a good example of the downside.

In handling transom power you need to consider the magnitude of side thrust *at maneuvering speeds,* particularly when power is applied astern. If it is considerable, you can handle the boat much as you would a conventional inboard. If side thrust is negligible, as it often will be, different techniques are required.

Single Drive

Let's begin our discussion with a single drive unit sans side thrust. For clarity, we'll illustrate with an outboard, but the operational differences between an outboard and a sterndrive are minor.

In Figure 19-1 we approach a float for a routine landing. We're coming in port side to in order to emphasize the differences between transom power and a single-screw inboard. The initial approach is essentially the same for all boats— 20 degrees or so off the face of the pier. How we handle the fine-tuning at (2) depends on the boat. If your boat answers the drive-unit "rudder" when you take it out of gear, you can turn the wheel as necessary to correct your heading. Chances are, however, you'll need prop thrust to exercise any appreciable steering control. The secret here is to avoid oversteering and use no more prop thrust than is required. Your immediate reaction will most likely be to turn the wheel harder if the boat doesn't respond to its rudder, but it is better to use less steering-wheel action, nudging the throttle in and out of gear to produce the desired result. I can't overemphasize this point: Transom-powered boats tend to understeer in neutral and oversteer in gear, and one of the biggest challenges in handling them is learning the balance of "rudder" and throttle necessary to produce the desired speed and heading without constant weaving. The knowledge will come with practice.

When you get close to the pier (3), put the "rudder" hard away (in this case right) to swing the stern in and bring the boat parallel to the pier. Ideally, you'll take the engine out of gear at this point and coast in; considering your lack of rudder action, however, some power may be necessary to effect the steering you desire. Here again, a delicate hand on the throttle will allow you to steer as you wish without coming in too fast. As you come alongside (4), use reverse to stop forward motion as in the situations discussed in previous chapters. The difference here is that you lack significant side thrust and thus have to turn the propeller toward the pier (left rudder) to help swing the stern in as you stop. Exactly how much left rudder is required depends on the degree of side thrust

Figure 19-1

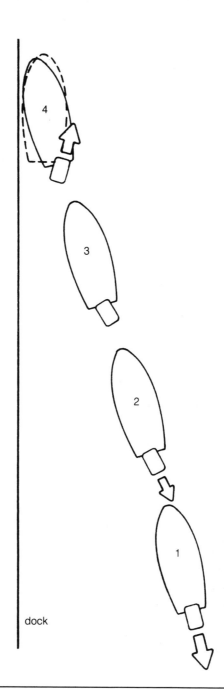

DOCKING WITH TRANSOM POWER

in the unit. Too much rudder causes too much stern swing, and vice versa. You'll have to experiment with your boat to learn how much it takes.

Since we are using directed main thrust to bring the stern in where we want it (rather than relying on side thrust as we did with inboards), landing starboard side to would be just as easy. All you'd have to do is swing the steering wheel the opposite way.

Twin Drives

Now let's see what happens with two drive units. There's no diagram for this one, because most dual-drive installations are simply single units used in pairs. Counter-rotation, the main ingredient in twin screw responses, was only recently introduced in outboards and sterndrives and is still far from common, which means you can usually handle twin transom power as if it were single. In fact, it is usually easiest to forget that you have a dual installation and do your docking maneuvers on one engine alone. This gives you enough power for control, and that's really all you need. The engine on the side away from the pier often gives you a slight advantage, but either will do.

When both props have the same rotation and the trim factors are set to reduce side thrust at cruising speeds, there is sometimes significant side thrust at maneuvering speeds with both engines in gear. If this is the case with your boat, you can dock your boat right side to as you would with a single-screw inboard—that is, by using reverse alone to swing the stern in as you stop. In fact, turning the drives toward the pier in this case would produce too much stern swing. You'll have to see for yourself. Of course, the advantage of transom power (and it's a decided one) is that even if this is the case, you can still dock wrong side to by turning the drives before you apply reverse.

Backing In

Because transom-powered boats are usually quite steerable in reverse, they can be backed into a slip easily. The difference is that turns must usually be aided with the steering wheel even if you have two units, since dual-drive installations seldom exhibit enough twin-screw action to be handled with throttles and clutches alone. You may also discover that transom-power side thrust will increase or diminish with a change in drive trim angle. If this is so with your boat, minimize side thrust before backing—it will make the job easier.

Figure 19-2 shows a typical maneuver with a single-drive unit. One of a pair would produce basically the same results. If you have a dual installation, you might want to experiment with coming in twin-screw style, but ultimately you're likely to stick with transom-power techniques.

Remember that the advice of Chapter 18 regarding allowance for wind and current applies here as well.

Trailering Techniques

They're not exactly docking techniques, but handling a trailer and getting your boat on and off it are often part of transom-powered boating, so let's look at these aspects also.

If your vehicle is suited to the task, towing a trailer is easy. You mainly have to remember that your vehicle is in effect a lot longer with trailer in tow, and it

Figure 19-2

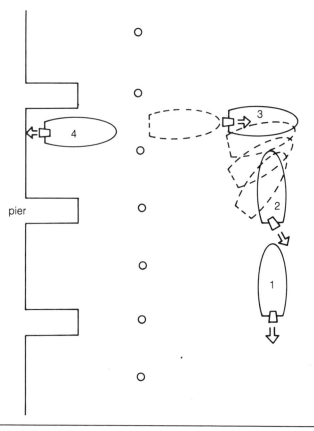

pier

BACKING WITH TRANSOM POWER

bends in the middle. This means taking wider turns and watching your clearance when you do turn. The fun comes when you back up (Figure 19-3). That bend in the middle can get you every time. To make the trailer back the way you want, you have to start backing your car the other way (2). Until that gets to be a habit, you'll have problems. Figure 19-4 shows a tip I learned years ago from a fellow boatman whose vocation was driving 18-wheelers. When going ahead, put your hand on the top of the steering wheel and move it in the direction of the desired turn. When backing, put your hand on the bottom of the wheel and do the same. It works.

Once you have the trailer turning the way you want it (Figure 19-3), turn the wheel the other way and follow the trailer back (3), straightening out when you're lined up on the ramp (4).

Before you back all the way, stop and get the trailer and boat ready for the launch. Disconnect the trailer tail lights, make sure docklines are made fast on the boat and ready to use, and *make sure the drain plug has been put in!* Then back the trailer as far as you need to, keeping in mind that you don't want your drive wheels to get onto the slippery part of the ramp. When you're in position, chock

Figure 19-3

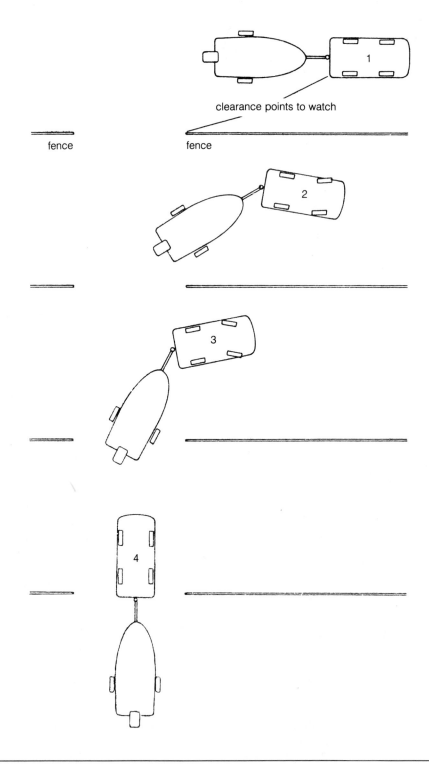

clearance points to watch

fence   fence

Figure 19-4

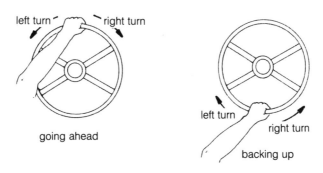

left turn — right turn

going ahead

left turn   right turn

backing up

BACKING TRACTOR TRAILER STYLE

your vehicle's rear wheels so it can't move back any farther, turn off the engine, and release the winch line from the boat's bow eye.

Depending on the angle of the ramp, the depth of the water (stage of tide in many areas), and the design of your boat and trailer, getting the boat off and floating can be as easy as a gentle shove or as difficult as backing it off with its own power. You'll probably run into every variation sooner or later. If you're able to push it off, you or a companion should have the bow line in hand, ready to secure to a pier as soon as the boat clears the trailer. If you have to power off, you can maneuver the boat back for an easy landing. All that remains then is to park the rig and get aboard!

Hauling the boat is equally easy. Again, you'll want to back in the trailer as far as you can without compromising the traction needed to pull it up the ramp. Many trailer boaters make sure the trailer's bunks are thoroughly wet before hauling, even if it requires backing farther—the boat slides better on wet bunks. Just be sure your towing vehicle's drive wheels are on a nonskid surface, and remember to chock the wheels before you begin hauling.

Getting the boat back on the trailer can be easier than getting it off. In fact, if the trailer is in enough water, you can run the boat right up onto it. Obviously, you should approach straight on, but even if you're slightly canted, the trailer's bunks will straighten out the boat as you slide on. The difficult part is learning how much power it takes to get onto the trailer, the trick being to approach slowly, get the bow onto the trailer, and then apply more power to complete the move. If you don't slide all the way on, hook up the winch cable and crank her the rest of the way (or use an electric winch if you want to take the easy way).

Be sure to trim the drive(s) to full trailer position before you drive up the ramp; then haul away. Once clear of the ramp area, complete the tiedown, plug in the trailer lights, check the area to make sure you haven't left anything behind, and away you go.

Some people think trailer boating is more work, and in some ways it is. On the other hand, you can load and unload directly from house to boat to house (as opposed to house to car to boat to car to house), and you can go boating in some interesting areas that are not directly accessible by water. You can also find more

Figure 19-5

THE JOYS OF A TRAILERABLE BOAT   *Keeping your boat on a trailer lets you launch her anywhere there's a ramp, opening the door to nearly unlimited boating opportunities. (Courtesy Calkins)*

Figure 19-6

A TRAILER BOAT HINT   *Launch 'N Load walkways make trailering easier by helping you keep your feet dry when you haul and launch. (Courtesy Wesbar Corporation)*

odd moments to take care of your boat when it is sitting in your driveway rather than docked even a few miles away, and you need not worry about painting the bottom to prevent marine growth. In short, if your boat is in the trailerable size range anyway, keeping it on a trailer can be the best answer all around.

◆

20. Using Springlines for Maneuvering

Several years ago I had to "parallel park" a 58-foot yachtfisherman into a tight berth on a nasty day. It was a hairy predicament with the wind blowing about 35 knots off the pier, very shallow water not far from its face, and just room enough (about 60 feet) to squeeze between two other boats. Definitely a get-it-right-the-first-try situation. In fact, if I'd had a choice, I wouldn't have tried at all! But it was the last available space in the marina, and the weather, bad as it was already, was deteriorating so rapidly that we didn't want to travel on. When we got settled and secured, I thanked the dockmaster for her help—and for letting us have the space. She commented that she had been " . . . turning people away all morning. But I let you come in because I saw you had a hand ready with a springline and were obviously prepared to make it OK."

I can't guarantee that proper use of springlines will get you dock space, but I can promise that it will help you get into—and out of—spaces with greater ease.

A Springline Taxonomy

Before we go through the techniques involved in using springlines, we should get together on what to call them. Convention decrees a two-part name. The first part refers to the direction in which the line leaves the boat; the second, to where it is made fast on the boat (Figure 20-1). That means a forward-bow spring leads forward from a cleat at or near the bow, while an after-bow spring runs aft from the same cleat. The same applies to forward- or after-quarter (or stern) springs. Larger boats have more possibilities, but in the size range of concern in this book, bow and quarter springs are probably all we need.

Who's on First

Over the years I have heard many discussions (arguments, even) as to whether you should make one end of the line fast to the boat and handle the free end on the pier or first secure the pier end and do your line handling on the boat. Which is it? At the risk of seeming wishy-washy, I have to say, "It all depends."

On ships, tugs, ferries, and large yachts, the pier end is usually made fast initially (often by dropping the loop of the eye over a bollard or piling), and the line handling is done by the crew aboard ship. This has created the impression among some observers that it is the only correct way. Nonsense. Rather, it is the better way for these situations because the vessels have the crew and working space to make it feasible. As we'll soon see, there are definite advantages to keeping full control of your lines in your own crew's hands.

Many small boats, on the other hand, barely have deck space for the cleat, to say nothing of room for a line handler. Then too, in many situations you have more available help (in both number and ability) from the dockhands than from your deckhands. In these cases, why not attach the line to the boat and do the handling on the pier? It not only makes sense, it is often the only option. Not as shippy, perhaps, but practical nonetheless.

Docking

The After-Bow Spring

An after-bow spring is the first line I put ashore 99.9 percent of the time when coming alongside a pier or float. This one line can act as the "poor man's bow thruster" and help you get alongside and, more important, stay alongside even if wind and current are doing their best to push you away. Figure 20-2 shows how it works. When you go forward against an after-bow spring, the line keeps the bow from going much ahead or (in this case) swinging to starboard despite the

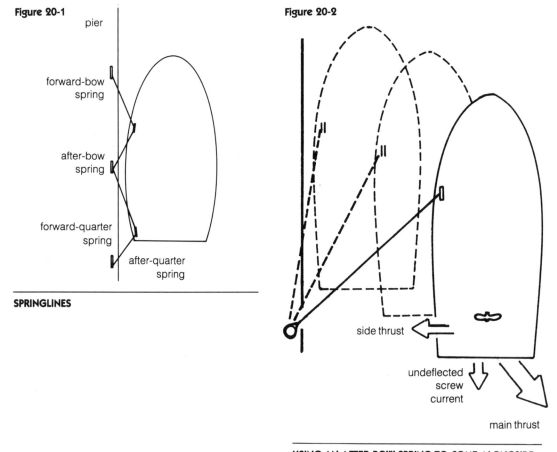

Figure 20-1

pier

forward-bow spring

after-bow spring

forward-quarter spring

after-quarter spring

SPRINGLINES

Figure 20-2

side thrust

undeflected screw current

main thrust

USING AN AFTER-BOW SPRING TO COME ALONGSIDE

propeller thrust and right rudder. This sets up a parallelogram of forces: Since the stern is swinging in and the bow can't swing away, the boat moves sideways.

A nice attribute of a well-placed after-bow spring is that you can nestle stationary against the pier on that one line so long as you leave the engine in gear with the rudder away from the pier. That means for short stops, such as to let someone run ashore for groceries or cold drinks, it's the only line you need. If you plan to stay awhile and thus will put out other lines, this spring will keep you snugly in place until the other lines are secured.

Essentially two factors control the way in which a boat moves sideways on an after-bow spring. One is the location of the cleat—the point on the boat to which it is made fast. Ideally, it will be just forward of straight abeam from the pivot point, which is usually about one-third of the boat's length aft of the bow. The other is the length of the line. Generally speaking, the longer the line, the more the stern swings in; the shorter the line, the more the bow comes in. If cleat location and line length are perfect, you'll slide almost exactly sideways and stay neatly in place, parallel to the pier, on one line alone.

Of course, if the spring is too long, you might run into the boat in front of you; the line has to be properly adjusted for safety even if doing so compromises its performance. Simply changing the point at which the line is made fast ashore can often make it "right" again, but you won't always have this option.

This brings us to the very-strong-wind-off-the-dock landing maneuver. The basic problem is that no matter how close you get to the pier before you stop, a very strong wind will begin to set you away almost immediately. You can *get* there, but *staying* there is another matter. However, if you get that springline ashore and made fast at both ends, you can't be set off any farther than the length of the line. The only problem is that the springline will often be too long for the available space because of the distance you drift before the line can be made fast at both ends. If you then use the spring to come all the way in, you'll hit the boat lying ahead of you.

The answer is to shorten the line in stages, a simple procedure though not an easy one. You must work your way in under forward power just as far as you dare, then ease slightly astern to create slack in the line. As soon as the slack appears, the line handler lets loose the working end, removes the slack, and then secures the line so you can once again go ahead on it. Most important: You have to do this very, very quickly before you drift out too far, or you won't gain a thing. Naturally, if the line is being handled aboard the boat, communicating with the line handler is easier, and you can give better warning of your intended throttle and clutch actions. That's a prime reason for making the boat end the working end whenever you can.

You may have to repeat the process many times to shorten the line enough to let you bring the boat alongside and into the available space. The more slack you remove each time, the quicker you'll get there, but you can't rush it. If you try to grab too much slack at once, you'll only drift farther away before you can retie the line, and you'll lose as much or perhaps more than you gained.

Figure 20-3

Figure 20-4

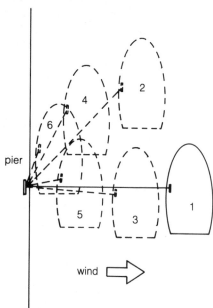

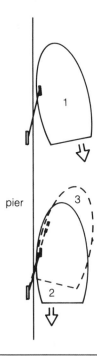

WORKING AGAINST THE WIND *An after-bow spring and a little patience can work near miracles in getting a boat against the pier when a strong wind is blowing you away.*

TWIN SCREWS AND THE AFTER-BOW SPRING *With the starboard engine ahead and the port engine in neutral, the stern swings out (1). With just the port engine ahead, the boat will remain at station and parallel to the pier (2) provided the spring is not too long, in which case the bow will swing out (3).*

The After-Bow Spring with Twin Screws

Using twins in conjunction with an after-bow spring gives you even more control over the boat's sideways movement. For example, the outboard (away from the pier) engine will tend to move the bow in faster, while the engine closer to the pier tends to bring the stern in first (Figure 20-4). When lying alongside, the inboard engine will usually hold you close and parallel to the pier, though if the line is too long, the bow will tend to swing out.

The Forward-Bow Spring

This one isn't quite so useful for getting to the pier, but it can help you stay there if for some reason (such as not having located something ashore to make fast to) you can't use an after-bow spring. Since you use power astern to make it work (Figure 20-5), the forward-bow spring can also be useful in preventing you from going too far when you have to back in to the berth or slip.

You can use a forward-bow spring and power to hold your boat in place without other lines in a manner similar to the after-bow spring (Figure 20-6). It

Figure 20-5

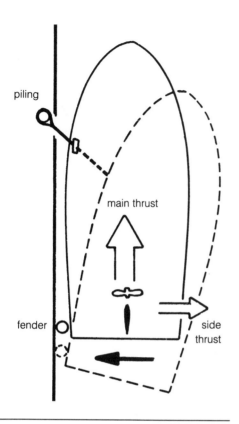

piling

main thrust

fender

side
thrust

BACKING IN AGAINST THE FORWARD BOW SPRING

Figure 20-6

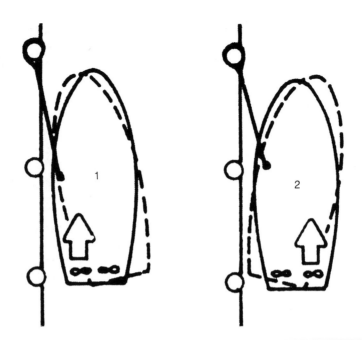

TWIN SCREWS AND THE FORWARD-BOW SPRING *When backing against the spring, the inside engine will hold the boat in place but allow the stern to swing slightly out; the outside engine will allow the bow to drift out.*

doesn't work quite as well, however, for two reasons. First, the length of a forward-bow spring is even more critical than that of an after-bow spring. The longer it is, the more the bow tends to swing out. This can be countered slightly in a twin screw by using only the inboard engine, but there is no solution to the second problem: Propellers running in reverse are not as well protected as those running ahead, so they are more prone to damage from flotsam and other debris.

Most of the time, bow springs are all you need to come in to a pier. Chapter 9 showed that control begins at the stern. If you can keep the bow from going where you don't want it to, you can usually get the stern to cooperate with little difficulty. Sometimes a quarter spring will help, but usually it's best not to restrain the stern while you need control. Remember, if the stern can't swing, you can't do much to make the bow move either. The exception arises when a strong current makes swinging the stern especially difficult, at which point you may need springs at both ends to keep close to the pier. Once you have experimented a few times and have a working grasp of the principles, you'll be able to use a combination of springs whenever conditions require.

So much for using springlines to get in. Now let's see how they can help us get out.

Getting Away

There are a number of ways to use springlines when leaving a berth, but we'll concern ourselves with the two primary techniques. One involves a bow spring and the other a quarter spring, and both work well; the choice depends primarily on whether you are going ahead or astern immediately after leaving the pier. Needless to say, one technique swings the stern clear first while the other moves the bow.

The After-Bow Spring

Figure 20-7 shows that the line that's so handy for getting in can be equally handy for getting out. Many times, all you have to do is swing the rudder toward the pier, and the stern will start moving away. If this isn't enough, and under some conditions it won't be, shortening the line will usually take care of things. Once the stern is far enough out, straighten the rudder, apply power astern, and back away.

With twin screws (Figure 20-8), go ahead on the outboard engine and, if necessary, back on the inboard. When the stern is angled sufficiently to clear the berth, put both engines astern and back away.

The after-bow spring will also work if you want to clear the berth going ahead. The limiting factor is initial maneuvering room astern. As long as you can back up even a little, the spring will usually let you get the stern far enough out to then

Figure 20-7

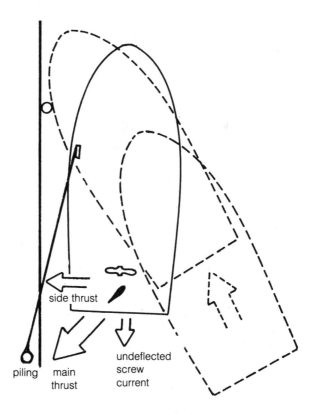

side thrust

piling   main thrust

undeflected screw current

LEAVING YOUR BERTH WITH AN AFTER-BOW SPRING: SINGLE-SCREW BOAT

swing it back in as you go ahead, pointing the bow away from the pier (Figure 20-9). If the after-bow spring was your first line ashore, making it the last line you cast off is usually easiest.

If you have no room astern, however, and the wind is making it difficult to get away, you may want to swing the bow out first. "How can I do that," you ask, "when nothing happens until the stern swings, and the stern *can't* swing through the pier?"

It's easy. Use a forward-quarter springline to create a new combination of forces that will *make* the bow swing out.

The Forward-Quarter Spring

When you apply power astern against a forward-quarter spring, you keep the pier side of the boat from moving back while the screw current tries its best to move the whole boat. Since it can't, it will move the free side, and since the pier prevents the stern from swinging inward as it does, the bow has to swing out (Figure 20-10). Leave the rudder amidship as you do this so that you'll be all set to go straight ahead when you apply forward power—which you should do as soon as the bow has swung out enough for a clean getaway.

With twin screws, you'll usually use just the outboard engine astern and then both ahead when it's time to go forward.

Figure 20-8

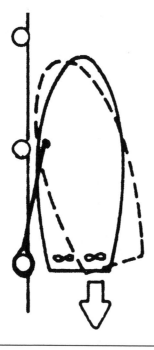

LEAVING YOUR BERTH WITH AN AFTER-BOW SPRING: TWIN-SCREW BOAT   *Initiate your swing away from the pier with the outside engine by running ahead against the spring.*

Mind Your Ps and Qs

Here we're talking about *protection* and *quickness*. When you use springlines to move away from a pier, the portion of your hull that is held to the pier by line tension will be subjected to considerable compression—especially when you use a forward-quarter spring. In both cases, but especially at the stern, be sure to use a substantial fender or two at the point of contact to protect your topsides.

Because springs are most useful when nature is trying to hold you against the pier (otherwise you could probably get away without them), you must make a quick transition from swinging out to moving away. That means shifting the clutch(es), engaging the throttle(s), and casting off the line with dispatch. Here are a couple of tricks to make things easier.

If you are working with a cleat on a pier or float, hook the eye of your springline over one horn of the cleat (Figure 20-11). Tension on the line will hold it in place while you are using it, yet it will come free (often, automatically) as soon as the boat starts moving the other way.

If you are working with a piling, secure the springline to the boat, then run it around the piling and back to the boat (Figure 20-12), where you secure it again. When the time comes to cast it off, you need only undo the second set of hitches to be clear, and you can pull the line aboard as you leave.

Figure 20-9

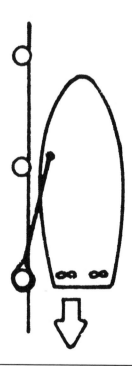

MOVING AHEAD ON AN AFTER-BOW SPRING   *If there is room to back up before this maneuver, the spring will permit you to swing the bow out (preparatory to leaving the berth) while moving ahead.*

Figure 20-10

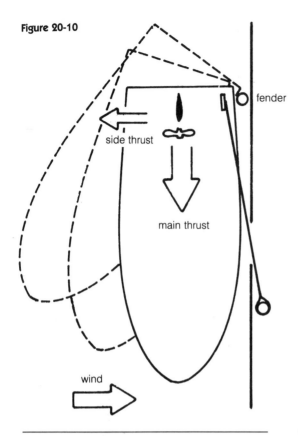

fender

side thrust

main thrust

wind

LEAVING YOUR BERTH WITH FORWARD-QUARTER SPRING

Figure 20-11

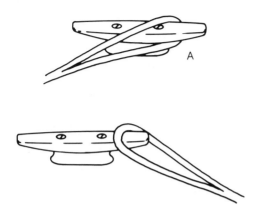

Figure 20-12

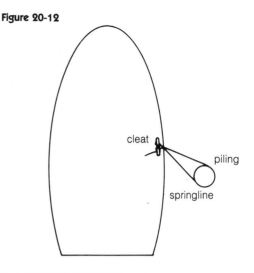

cleat

piling

springline

A QUICK RELEASE FOR CLEATS *With the eye looped over one horn of the cleat, it will hold well under strain while the boat pivots (A), yet release easily when tension is relaxed.*

A QUICK RELEASE FOR PILINGS *When you secure both ends of a springline at the boat, releasing one end will free the line from the piling even when it is out of reach.*

This chapter has really only scratched the surface of maneuvering with spring-lines. The more you work with them, the more you become aware of the kind of help you can expect from different lines as well as when and how to use them.

———————◆———————

21• Using Docklines

One of the saddest sights to me is a beautiful boat tied up with a rat's nest of docklines. It not only looks terrible, it can be hazardous—for improperly secured docklines may not be secure at all. And it's such a shame, because doing it right is usually easier than doing it wrong.

A correct dockline configuration comprises the proper number of adequately sized lines deployed in directions that will best hold the boat in place despite nature's attempts to move her. The exact arrangement will vary with the circumstances, but the basics are universal. As you'll discover, rigging proper mooring lines for your boat involves only a few simple principles and a knowledge of how and when to apply them. The better you know the how, the less trouble you'll have with the when.

In the Slip

Five or six lines are usually all you need to hold a boat securely in a slip. In Figure 21-1 we see that the lines from the bow (A) prevent side-to-side movement forward, and if the pilings are far enough ahead of the boat, they also prevent it from moving very far back. When the pilings are closer to the bow, a forward-bow spring (B) prevents backward movement. The crossed stern lines (C) hold the after section laterally but won't stop forward movement totally because they scissor. However, an after spring (D or D1, you would seldom need both) will do that job.

Since the load is spread rather evenly over five or six working lines, you'll rarely have to add more or double up. In a strong blow from starboard, a breastline straight out to a dock, piling, or even an anchor would take some of the strain off the starboard bow and stern lines. If you do double up for security, be sure to equalize the length of the lines to balance the load, or the added lines won't help much: The shorter line will overload before the longer line takes much strain.

Alongside

Three or four lines will hold a boat alongside a float or pier (Figure 21-2). As mentioned in the last chapter, we generally put out the after-bow spring (A) first because it can help us come alongside and hold us there until we get the other lines set. Since we want to maintain control until we no longer need it, leave the stern free to swing and put out the bow line (B) second. When that is set, add the stern line (C). Please note that it should go ashore from the outboard cleat.

If the bow line is long enough (thus making an acute angle with the dock), it will keep you from sliding back. A shorter bow line calls for a forward-quarter spring (D).

If you feel the need for greater security, you can spread the load to six lines by adding another bow line (E), which is preferably rigged to a cleat not used by the bow line, and another stern line (F). As in Figure 21-1, a strong blow from starboard would suggest another line or two in that direction.

Considering Tide

If your docklines are long enough and cut a good angle, they will usually work for either fixed or floating piers—at least in the most commonly encountered tidal ranges. If you should venture to an area of extreme range, just pay attention to what local boatmen are doing. Amply long docklines coupled with a single breastline to the pier may do the trick. The breastline is kept snug and adjusted periodically with the tide to keep the boat close alongside while the other lines are slack.

One way to simplify dockline handling is with a permanent set at your home berth. You can cut them to the exact length you need for that location, with eyes on the boat ends. When you come in you need only pick up the lines and slip the eyes over your cleats, and you're all set. It's quick and easy. You then keep your other lines stowed to use only when you visit marinas, waterfront restaurants,

Figure 21-1

Figure 21-2

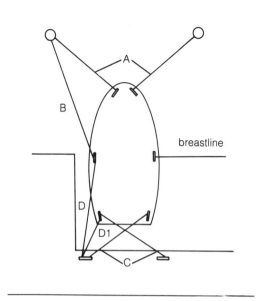

breastline

LINES FOR SLIP DOCKING

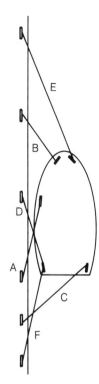

LINES FOR LYING ALONGSIDE A FLOAT OR PIER

and other locations. Permanent lines add expense, but the time and effort they save can be well worth it.

Now that we've seen how to deploy docklines, let's take a closer look at the gear involved. When it comes to the lines themselves, there are two criteria for "big enough." One is working strength (Figure 21-3), which will generally put you in the ballpark. However, modern synthetics are very strong for their size, so you can have sufficient strength in a line that is otherwise too small. For example, in mooring lines you have to consider abrasion and comfort in handling. A smaller line will wear down more quickly than a larger one because there is less bearing surface, and because the line has less diameter to begin with, nicks, scrapes, and general wear take a proportionately greater toll than they do on thicker line. A $1/16$-inch deep cut leaves about 90 percent strength in a $5/8$-inch line but only 80 percent in a $3/8$-inch line. If the $5/8$-inch line was oversized to begin with, 90 percent working strength is probably adequate, but if the $3/8$-inch line was just right, 80 percent won't be enough. Then, too, larger line is easier on the hands. Smaller sizes tend to cut into human flesh if there is much strain involved—and there can be under many conditions. Within practical limits, the larger the line, the better the grip you can get. One of the most unfortunate practical limits is your deck hardware. Many boatbuilders choose sizes that will look good on the

Figure 21-3

SIZE		MANILA		POLYPROPYLENE (Monofilament)		NYLON	
Dia.	Cir.	Breaking test (lbs.)	Lbs. per 100 ft.	Breaking test	Lbs. per 100 ft.	Breaking test	Lbs. per 100 ft.
1/4″	3/4″	600	2.0	1,250	1.2	1,650	1.5
5/16″	1″	1,000	2.9	1,900	1.8	2,550	2.5
3/8″	1 1/8″	1,350	4.1	2,700	2.8	3,700	3.5
7/16″	1 1/4″	1,750	5.25	3,500	3.8	5,000	5.0
1/2″	1 1/2″	2,650	7.5	4,200	4.7	6,400	6.5
5/8″	2″	4,400	13.3	6,200	7.5	10,400	10.5
3/4″	2 1/4″	5,400	16.7	8,500	10.7	14,200	14.5
13/16″	2 1/2″	6,500	19.5	9,900	12.7	17,000	17.0
7/8″	2 3/4″	7,700	22.5	11,500	15.0	20,000	20.0
1″	3″	9,000	27.0	14,000	18.0	25,000	26.0
1 1/16″	3 1/4″	10,500	31.3	16,000	20.4	28,800	29.0
1 1/8″	3 1/2″	12,000	36.0	18,300	23.7	33,000	34.0
1 1/4″	3 3/4″	13,500	41.8	21,000	27.0	37,500	40.0
1 5/16″	4″	15,000	48.0	23,500	30.5	43,000	45.0
1 1/2″	4 1/2″	18,500	60.0	29,700	38.5	53,000	55.0
1 5/8″	5″	22,500	74.4	36,000	47.5	65,000	68.0
1 3/4″	5 1/2″	26,500	89.5	43,000	57.0	78,000	83.0
2″	6″	31,000	108.0	52,000	69.0	92,000	95.0
		20% of breaking test		**17% of breaking test**		**11% of breaking test**	

RECOMMENDED WORKING LOADS

THE STRENGTH OF ROPE   *The tensile strength of new, unused rope is determined according to Cordage Institute standard test methods. The working loads recommended in the table are based on rope in good condition with appropriate splices, and should not be exceeded without expert knowledge of conditions and a professional assessment of the risks. The working loads shown are for twisted rope; recommended working loads for braided rope are 15 to 20 percent of tensile strength. (Courtesy Cordage Institute)*

boat, and this means that smaller boats get shortchanged. Too often, you cannot use the most appropriate size of line because it is too big for the hardware. Do the best you can.

What about length? For bow lines, I generally recommend the distance from the bow cleat to just ahead of the prop(s)—measured through the water. This is the length you'll end up with if you drop the line overboard, so why not start that way? Stern lines can be a bit shorter, but you might make them as long as the bow lines for interchangeability. Springlines should be longer, but exactly how long depends on such variables as tidal range, whether you'll moor to fixed or floating piers, etc. Twice the length of your boat will not be far out of line except for a few unusual circumstances (a very small boat in a great tidal range on a fixed pier would require longer, for example). If you mark the bitter ends, you can tell at a glance which line is which. I put one turn of whipping twine on the ends of the shortest lines, two turns on the medium, and three on the long. Tightly bound turns of electrical tape will work as well.

While line stowage can be a problem, carrying two for each cleat will allow you to double up in severe weather. The added safety factor justifies the effort.

As for fiber, there's only one practical choice: nylon. Natural fibers rot too quickly if not cared for properly. Dacron doesn't stretch enough, and polypropylene suffers from exposure to ultraviolet rays. Commercial boats often use polypro for large-diameter line where the added weight of nylon could make a difference in handling. They also subject their lines to so much wear that replacement is necessary before ultraviolet damage can take its toll. Chances are you won't have the same conditions, so stick with nylon.

There is also a choice between ordinary three-stranded twisted construction and braided line. I confess to straddling, though I like braided more and more as time goes by. Three-strand costs less, but braided is stronger size for size. Braided is more flexible and easier to handle, though it doesn't wear quite as well, the outer braid being more susceptible to damage from rough surfaces. Braided has slightly less stretch, but the difference is negligible—it's still nylon and still offers the shock absorber effect. Braided line also seems harder to splice, though once you learn how it really isn't. Ultimately the choice is one of personal preference.

All lines will last longer if you use chafing gear, including hardware in the form of chocks, hawsepipes, or fairleads wherever line must change direction. If a line doesn't lead directly from boat cleat to shore, you need one of the above. Make sure hardware surfaces are completely smooth inside and out (some have hidden sharp edges and can do more harm than good) and that the radius is compatible with both the diameter of the line and the bend it must make around the device. The sharper the bend, the larger the radius. If you have a sportfisherman or other boat in which the stern cleats are recessed in the cockpit, pay particular attention to how the stern lines will lead as they exit the boat. If the fairleads are in the aft ends of the covering boards (the sportfisherman's equivalent of narrow side decks between cockpit coaming and rail), a single stern cleat to port and one to starboard will work fine. If the fairleads are in the sides of the boat, it is better to have two on each side—one in the transom and one on the topside quarter (possibly with an accompanying cleat for each) . This will allow you to run stern lines in any fashion and use forward-stern springs without having to go around the corner of the transom.

Your lines will last longer if you add chafing gear at every point of potential wear. You can use storebought devices such as guards and tape or the less attractive, equally effective, and less expensive alternative, lengths of split hose.

Don't forget chafing gear, otherwise known as *fenders*, for the boat itself. The determining factors for size are the weight and windage of your boat. Select fenders with sufficient diameter to provide reserve protection after they have

Figure 21-4

CHAFING GEAR *Chafing gear can be as simple as a piece of hose slid over the line and tied, stitched, or otherwise seized in place.*

Figure 21-5

THE WELL-COVERED FENDER SET *Fenders are a bit like pocket change—you can almost never have too much of a good thing.*

Figure 21-6

FENDER BOARD *A fender board will protect a hull against pilings better than a single fender. As the tide goes up and down and the boat moves forward and back in her slip, some portion of the board will always remain between hull and piling.*

compressed under the load of your boat and whatever is pushing it against the pier or piling. Depending on the berth, you may need from two to four to provide adequate protection for a boat more than 22 feet long. This means carrying a minimum of four fenders (leaving your other side to the other guy if necessary) to a maximum of eight. Six should cover you well most of the time.

If you often have pilings between you and the pier, consider carrying fender boards in addition to fenders, especially if there is much range to the tide. Hang one fender board (which may or may not have some padding of its own) between the piling and a pair of fenders, and you'll be thoroughly protected as the tide rises and falls, even if the boat shifts slightly forward or aft in the process.

Finally, consider protection for the fenders. Most of them are made of a soft white plastic that soils with use. While there are fender cleaners on the market, it's easier to use washable cloth covers to keep your fenders pristine.

Getting Attached

Now that we've discussed the principles and the gear, let's look at the details—the little points to consider in doing a truly professional job of securing a boat.

The cleat is the most common object you'll find for attaching a line, yet it's amazing how often the task is done incorrectly. Usually you have only to drop the eye over the cleat. If you suspect that the eye may pop free, however, a couple of precautions will make sure it won't. The first (Figure 21-7) is more difficult to undo, but it holds well even when there's no strain on the line. I recommend it especially for those times when you attach the line to the boat and work the shore end. Just push the whole eye through the space between the mounting bolts and drop it back over the horns.

The second (Figure 21-8) is better for eye-ashore handling. Simply loop the eye around the cleat twice before putting any strain on the line. This way, a slack line can be flipped off the cleat from on deck, yet a line under strain cannot come undone accidentally.

Figure 21-7

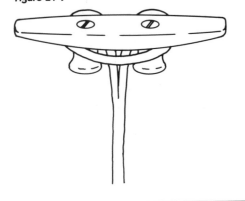

ONE WAY TO BELAY AN EYE TO A CLEAT

Figure 21-8

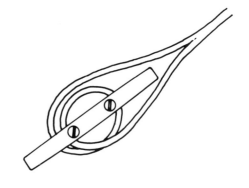

ANOTHER WAY TO MAKE FAST AN EYE TO A CLEAT

Now for the belaying of a working end with no eye (Figure 21- 9). Remember, always put one turn around the base first. This ensures that *both* sides of the cleat (horns and mounting bolts) share the load. Then take two or three crisscross (figure-eight) turns—the exact number depending on the relationship of line size to cleat size—and finish with a half hitch that follows the same pattern as the crisscross windings. This allows a relatively easy release even if the line has been under abnormal strain. If you need to shorten the line, simply undo the hitch, back off the riding turns, take up the slack, and then belay it again. Any other cleat belay will one day force you to cut a jammed line to get it free.

Figure 21-9

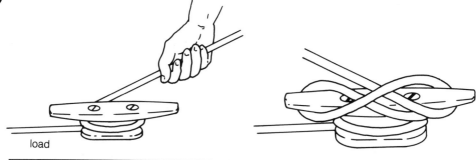

PROPER BELAYING OF A LINE THAT DOES NOT TERMINATE IN AN EYE *Always apply a round turn first; finish with a half hitch.*

Piling It Up

Pilings are also easy to attach to. If the eyes of your docklines are big enough, you can drop them over the pilings and work the other ends on your boat. However, the eyes of many commercially available docklines are too small to do this. You can fashion a bigger loop by passing the standing part of the line through the eye or by tying a bowline (Figure 21-10) in one end of the line. Passing the end through the eye to form a loop may seem easier, but it will snug up under tension and probably leave you more firmly attached than you would prefer. The bowline loop can be flipped off with ease.

If there is already another line on the piling, be sure to dip your line's eye through the eye of the other line (Figure 21-11). This way, either line can be removed without disturbing the other.

Figure 21-10

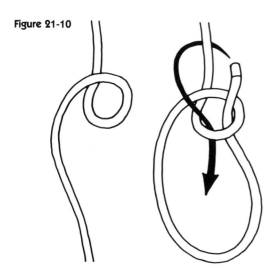

THE BOWLINE—AS NEAR TO ALL-PURPOSE AS A KNOT CAN BE

Figure 21-11

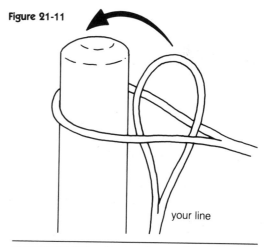

your line

DIPPING THE EYE *Putting the eye of your line up through the eye of a line that's already on the piling allows either line to be removed without disturbing the other.*

When putting a line *over* a piling is impossible, you'll have to use one of two other methods to make the line fast after you pass it *around* the piling. One is a clove hitch on the piling (Figure 21-12). Pass the end *under* the standing part, then around the piling again. The free end then goes *under* the most recent turn. The clove hitch is fine for short layovers, but it has two drawbacks. First, it must be under constant tension or it can come undone by itself. Second, if it comes under too much tension, a clove hitch can be nearly impossible to undo. Supplementing the clove hitch with a half hitch around the standing part alleviates the first drawback but not the second. A better method is to take a couple of turns around the piling and then a couple of half hitches or a clove hitch around the standing part (Figure 21-13).

Figure 21-12

Figure 21-13

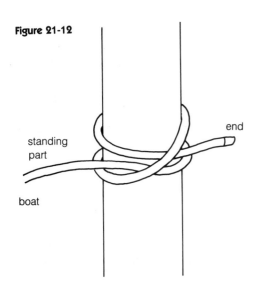

standing
part

end

boat

THE CLOVE HITCH *Pass the end of the line around the piling and* under *the standing part. Then pass it around again, over the first turn, tucking the end under the start of the second turn.*

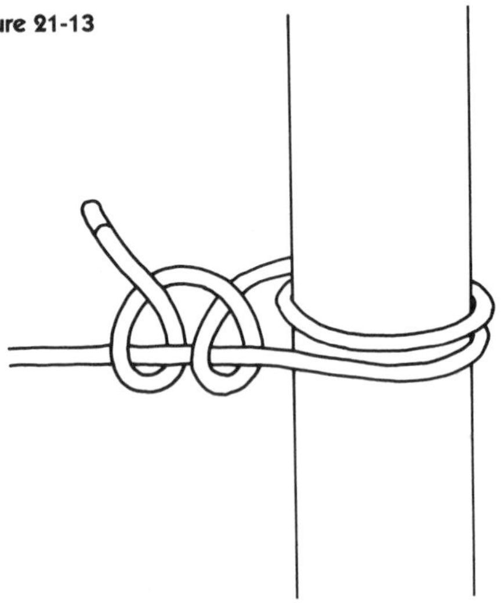

CLOVE HITCH ON THE STANDING PART *Sometimes putting a clove hitch on a piling is not such a good idea. Another option is to take a couple of turns around the piling then tie a clove hitch on the standing part.*

There are hundreds of knots you can learn if you wish, but all you need are the bowline, the clove hitch, the half hitch, and the cleat belay. If you learn these techniques well, you'll have no trouble securing your boat at any pier.

———————◆———————

22·Anchors and Anchoring Techniques

In the two previous chapters, we've assumed that your destination will always include a place to tie up. You can go boating that way, of course, but if you limit your trips to cruising from one marina to another you'll miss a lot of fun, because one of the great pleasures our sport offers is the ability to get away from it all. Though we were all born too late to venture boldly where no one has ever gone before (at least on this planet), we still have the opportunity to visit where others seldom go. And that calls for "hanging off the hook."

Choosing an Anchor

Anchors so typify boating that we use them as symbols of our sport—putting them on hats and blazers to announce to the world that we are involved with the sea. Anchors have been a part of boating since nearly the beginning, and for centuries they changed very little. In fact, boats changed more than anchors did. Through all that time, weight was the prime consideration. The heavier, the better.

But with the development of the modern anchor, most notably the Danforth lightweight type (circa World War II), things changed drastically. The shape of the modern anchor enables it to penetrate the bottom and hold by strength rather than weight. So now, when choosing an anchor, we have to consider "which type?" in addition to "how big?"

Anchor Type

The best place to start the anchor-selection process is at ground level. Rocks, sand, clay, mud, coral, kelp, and other substances, along with various admixtures, form the bottoms of our anchorage areas. No two are identical, and no one anchor works best in all bottoms. So the type of anchor you'll use requires that you first consult a chart to determine what type of bottom you'll be anchoring in. Usually one type predominates in a particular area. Base your selection of a primary anchor on your home ground, with a nod to what you'll encounter when you go cruising. The anchors used by the majority of boatmen in your area were most likely chosen because they work. If you buy your boat from a knowledgeable local dealer, you can usually trust his advice in this matter, too. He should know what other customers are using, and why.

But as in other purchasing situations, the more you know, the better able you are to make an intelligent decision. So let's examine a few of the currently available anchor types to see how they fit in the real world.

Yachtsman (Figure 22-1). These are the old-fashioned anchors commonly used as symbols. They hold in rocks, where penetration (the claim to fame of newer varieties) is impossible, and they may gain a purchase in grassy bottoms which, again, Danforths and plows may fail to penetrate. But they are awkward to handle, and since they must be comparatively large to have sufficient weight for holding power, they aren't easy to stow. Unless you spend a lot of time in rocky areas and have a salty-looking old-fashioned yacht you don't want to "spoil" with a modern contrivance, best let them be decorative.

Navy-type (Figure 22-2).   These anchors don't belong on small boats. Sure, they come in small-boat sizes and look shippy, but unless they're very large, stockless anchors are not much good. Their main virtue is that being stockless, the shank can be drawn up into a hawsepipe, which is fine for ships and large yachts. Pound for pound (or fluke size for fluke size—a better correlation), they don't hold as well as the yachtsman.

Danforth (Figure 22-3).   These granddaddies of all modern anchors still have a lot going for them. Their holding power (in the right bottom) goes *far* beyond mere weight, particularly in the Hi-Tensile series. They can lie flat in deck chocks or lockers, so stowage and handling are relatively easy. They work best in solid mud, clay, or hard-packed sand, where they can burrow unbelievably deep in very short order if set with sufficient scope.

They become less efficient as bottom density lessens and don't work as well in soft sand or near-liquid mud. Because they depend on penetration (a result of fluke angle), kelp, grass, or other weeds can prevent them from taking hold even if the bottom beneath the weeds is ideal. They are nearly useless in rocks.

Figure 22-1

THE YACHTSMAN'S ANCHOR   *Good for anchoring in rocks, but not the best choice for all-around use. The one shown here is small and light; you'd be more apt to see a 50-pounder on a boat over 30 feet long.*

A Danforth depends so much on the angle of pull against its flukes that when this angle changes, the anchor can come out of the bottom. Thus, Danforths are prone to losing their grip when your boat swings on a change of wind or tide. When the anchor is easy to set initially—no kelp or other hindrance—it will usually reset itself with no problem. If there is *any* hindrance to easy reentry, however, it will most likely start to drag. But the Danforth is still a prime choice for general use.

Danforth followers. The success of the Danforth anchor both in use and in the marketplace has prompted a number of clones and derivatives. Some of the clones look so much like Danforths you have to check the shank to be sure. If it looks like a Danforth but doesn't say so, beware! Imitators usually use a different fluke angle to avoid patent infringement and may not achieve proper penetration.

Derivatives are another story. Danforths, as good as they are, suffer the fate of many pioneers. The trail they blazed has been followed by others who had no intention of imitating (a form of flattery closely resembling rip-off) but rather chose to improve upon progressive thinking.

Fortress anchors (Figure 22-4) are one example. Fabricated of a hardened, marine-grade aluminum-magnesium-silicon alloy, they take the strength-with-

Figure 22-2

THE STOCKLESS OR "NAVY" ANCHOR *Though these anchors come in small-boat sizes, they are best suited to large yachts where they can be hauled up into a hawsepipe with a mechanical windlass. They have to be heavy to work well.*

lightness concept to the nth degree. My experience with them has been limited, but reports—including one released by the U.S. Navy—and their use by many well-known megayachts—including transatlantic speed-record-setter *Gentry Eagle* —suggest they are well worth considering.

Plow or CQR. There are several varieties, all having a single fluke. This practically eliminates dislodging when the boat swings, since a single fluke will better follow the rode—a tendency encouraged by one of several design variations depending on the brand you choose.

The original CQR plow (Figure 22-5) uses a hinge to pivot the shank. The Bruce anchor (Figure 22-6; its manufacturers don't call it a plow, the single fluke being less plow-shaped than that of the CQR) relies on shape alone—the side humps work to reposition it after a swing.

A relatively new entry from the manufacturers of the CQR is the Delta (Figure 22-7). It incorporates aspects of each of the other plows and boasts two special abilities. One, it is designed to freefall unattended—which makes it especially good for pulpit/automatic-windlass applications. Two, no matter how it lands, it will always flip over to the proper attitude for best penetration.

In my experience, a single-fluke anchor holds better in sand than a double-fluke anchor, and while no anchor is *great* in grass or weed, the single-fluke type

Figure 22-3

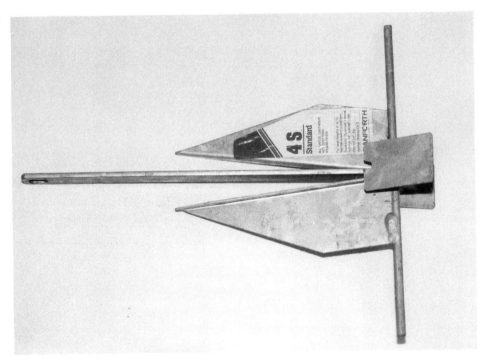

THE DANFORTH ANCHOR   *The granddaddy of all modern anchors, it holds well in most bottoms. Beware of imitations; if you want a Danforth, be sure it says Danforth.*

usually gets through and holds better. The main drawback to single-fluke anchors is that they don't stow as easily, but they are perfect to hang from a pulpit.

Anchor Size

Total load, not merely the overall length of the boat, is the critical factor for determining anchor size. A high-sided family cruiser with a lot of gear aboard will need more holding power than a low-profile, center console fisherman or sportboat of equal length. Keep this in mind when you look at manufacturers' guidelines.

Keep in mind too that while anchor weight is no longer the sole factor in holding power, it still matters. That is, within a given brand and style of anchor,

Figure 22-4

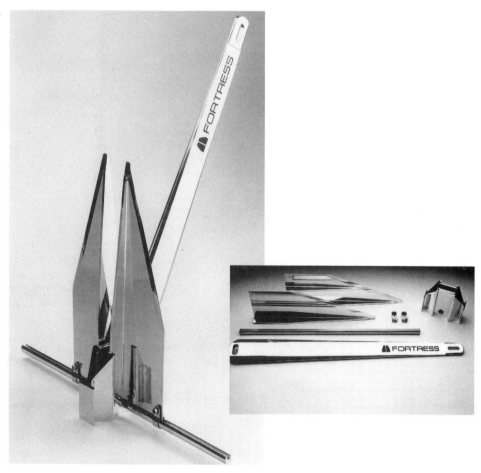

THE FORTRESS ANCHOR *The lightweight principle carried to the nth degree. These aluminum alloy anchors hold exceptionally well by design rather than weight. (Courtesy Fortress)*

the larger (heavier) it is, the better it holds, and the better it is able to penetrate the bottom under adverse conditions. So when you consult the manufacturers' tables for recommended sizes, if you must err, do so on the large side. Then, too, consider that we should be talking in the plural. One anchor isn't enough. There are times when you'll need two just to keep in proper position (we'll see how in just a bit), and because anchors are part of your safety gear, a backup is good insurance.

The old admonition to carry a lunch hook, a working anchor, and a storm anchor is still valid. The theory is that your lunch hook can be light, small, and easy to handle because you'll use it only when the weather is good and you're anchoring for a short time. Chances are someone will be aboard to keep an eye on things, so you don't need the full security of a heftier anchor.

Figure 22-5

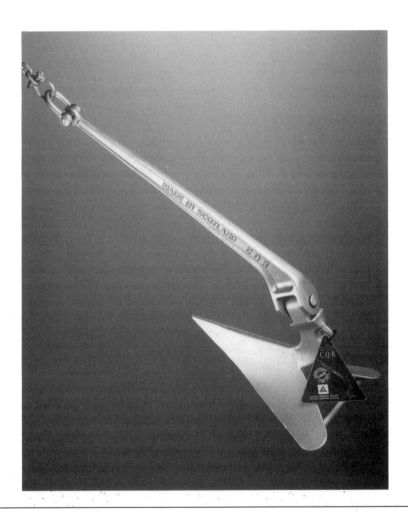

THE CQR PLOW   *Particularly good for anchoring where weed or grass hinder bottom penetration. (Courtesy Jay Stuart Haft)*

Using one that's easy to set and weigh makes anchoring more pleasurable, and some anchors especially designed for lunch-hook use have quick-release mechanisms for even easier removal from the bottom. This is nice, but it's possible to rig your own quick-release on any anchor (see below).

A working anchor should be large enough to hold under average-to-good conditions—such as anchoring overnight in mildly disagreeable weather. As its name implies, your storm anchor should be the big gun for really nasty conditions.

After suggesting that the old rule of thumb has merit, I'll acknowledge that carrying, stowing, and using three anchors can be physically impractical on many of today's powerboats. So, as we get on with other aspects of your ground tackle system, I'll show you how to make two do the work of three. But first, let's look at the rest of the system, because anchors don't work by themselves.

Figure 22-6

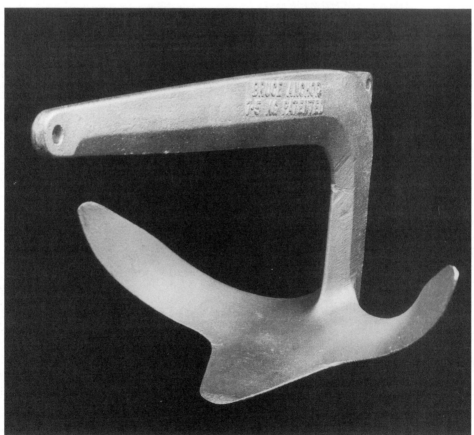

THE BRUCE ANCHOR   *A variation on the plow theme, but with no moving parts. Good for most bottoms and well suited to hanging from pulpits. (Courtesy Imtra Corp.)*

Figure 22-7

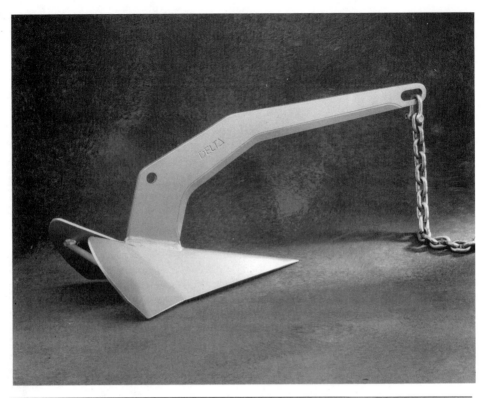

THE DELTA ANCHOR   *More "plow-like" than the Bruce, but still with no moving parts. A relative newcomer from the manufacturer of the CQR, the Delta is intended for lighter duty than the plow. (Courtesy Jay Stuart Haft)*

Ground Tackle

The anchor line, or rode, does more than connect the anchor to the boat. Properly employed, it also helps the anchor hold—particularly anchors that depend on fluke angle for penetration. Generally speaking, modern anchors need the pull against them to be as close to horizontal as possible. Obviously, unless you are anchoring a submarine, a truly horizontal pull is out of the question. However, we can approach it through catenary action and *scope* (the ratio of rode length to water depth—Figure 22-8).

An all-chain anchor rode is the most secure option. The added weight (as compared with a similar length of rope), greater breaking strength, resistance to abrasion, and natural catenary action make it superior on all counts. But a chain rode is not always practical. Many small pleasureboats can't carry that much extra weight up forward. Even if yours can, hauling chain back aboard is a royal pain unless you have a windlass. The standard compromise is a short length of chain (anywhere from 6 to 40 feet) between the anchor and a fiber (usually nylon) rode. This provides chafe protection for the part of the rode that can be expected to

Figure 22-8

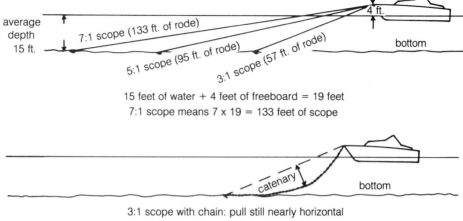

15 feet of water + 4 feet of freeboard = 19 feet
7:1 scope means 7 x 19 = 133 feet of scope

3:1 scope with chain: pull still nearly horizontal

SCOPE AND CATENARY ACTION   *With a combination chain-and-fiber rode, a scope of 7:1 or better produces the near horizontal pull required by anchors—especially if wind and wave action put a lot of strain on the line. An all-chain rode, being heavier, produces a sag, or catenary, between boat and anchor. This acts as a shock absorber whenever wind and wave cause the boat to tug against the rode, and the pull on the anchor remains more nearly horizontal even with shorter scope.*

come in contact with the bottom and adds weight to the end of the line to help keep the pull on the anchor more nearly horizontal.

Because chain can rust—which not only is unsightly but also causes stains—and can scratch shiny gelcoat, many boatmen opt for vinyl-covered chain. The covering protects the chain from rusting (for a while, at least) and protects the boat from being scratched by the metal. In my opinion, however, the commercially available vinyl-covered chains are too short (often about 3 feet). I suggest you buy at least 6 feet of proper-sized chain (the more the better) and then coat it yourself if you wish. The vinyl coating is available in liquid form at most marine stores and is not difficult to apply.

Since part of the chain's purpose is to add weight to the end of the rode, you should err on the large side. If you have a small boat, strong enough may not be heavy enough.

Don't shortchange yourself on the rest of the rode either. It should be long enough to provide optimum scope for your intended anchorages, and large enough in diameter to be easy on the hands and resistant to chafing. This often means a bigger line than working-load tables alone would suggest. How long should it be? I've already alluded to the importance of scope, and we'll cover it more thoroughly when we get to anchoring techniques. An average scope of 7:1 is a good place to start. That means that to anchor in 10 feet of water, you'll need a minimum of 70 feet of rode. My recommendation for coastal cruisers is 300 feet, this being enough for most situations. Obviously, if your boat's rope locker can't carry that much, you have to pare it down. But anchor rode, like money, falls in the never-too-much category. Carry as much as you have room for; eventually you'll be glad you did.

Figure 22-9A

WIND SPEED	BOAT LENGTH (FT.)												
	10	15	20	25	30	35	40	50	60	70	80	90	100
15 kts.	40	60	90	125	175	225	300	400	500	675	900	1200	1600
30 kts.	160	250	360	490	700	900	1200	1600	2000	2700	3600	4800	6400
42 kts.	320	500	720	980	1400	1800	2400	3200	4000	5400	7200	9600	12,800
60 kts.	640	1000	1440	1960	2800	3600	4800	6400	8000	10,800	14,400	19,200	25,600

TYPICAL GROUND TACKLE HORIZONTAL LOADS *Working loads (in pounds) placed on anchors and ground tackle as a function of boat size and wind speed. (Courtesy American Boat and Yacht Council)*

Figure 22-9B

Length	Anchor weight (based on plow or CQR)	Chain diameter	Rode diameter (figures for three-strand nylon)
Up to 21 ft.	18 lbs.	1/4 in.	7/16 in.
22–25	22	5/16	9/16
26–30	27	5/16	9/16
31–34	31	5/16	9/16
35–41	35	3/8	3/4
42–50	44	3/8	3/4

RECOMMENDED ANCHOR WEIGHTS, RODE SIZES, AND CHAIN SIZES FOR YACHTS BETWEEN 21 AND 50 FEET LONG *Using Figures 22-9A and 21-3, one would conclude that a 50-foot boat in a 42-knot blow needs a rode of 1- to 1 1/8-inch diameter, not 3/4-inch as this table indicates. But keep in mind that the breaking strength (as opposed to the recommended normal working load) of 3/4-inch nylon rode is 14,200 pounds, and in a 42-knot blow one would want to share the load between two anchors. (From* Anchoring, *by Brian Fagan. International Marine, 1986)*

Deck Gear

These days, many small boats (even some in the 20-foot range) sport the bow pulpit, electric windlass, and permanently mounted anchor once associated exclusively with large yachts. Believe me, such a system makes the task of anchoring much easier, often allowing you to set and weigh your anchor with almost no physical effort. There are other pluses, too. The windlass and pulpit allow you to use an all-chain rode, if your boat can carry the load, and eliminate the need for a lunch hook, since handling your main anchor is so easy. In fact, with the help of a windlass and pulpit, your heaviest anchor can be your normal working anchor. Your spare can then be lighter and thus easier to handle on those occasions when two anchors are needed.

Figure 22-10

(cont.
next
page)

Figure 22-10
(cont.)

FROM THE PULPIT   *Pulpit and windlass setups like those in the two bow shots have been common for years, but now we're beginning to see the idea in smaller boats. Though it hasn't yet been rigged, the Donzi, a 23-foot center-console fisherman, sports a built-in pulpit.*

Setting the Anchor

We'll start with a single anchor, since that will do for most situations. Before you set the anchor, seek out a good spot, meanwhile evaluating conditions of wind, water, bottom, and traffic in the anchorage. Among the questions you should answer before anchoring: How deep is the water? Will the water get deeper or shallower while you ride to anchor? Which way is the wind blowing, and is current a factor? How much swinging room do you have and will your swing change when the tide changes? Are there rocks or other shallow hazards you might swing over? Are there other anchored boats to consider? And finally, in view of the answers to the other questions, where do you want the anchor to be? Remember, this is *not* where your boat will end up; you have to allow for scope and lower your anchor far enough ahead of where you want to sit so that when you fall back on the rode, you'll be in the right place. It's less complicated than it sounds, and with very little practice you'll know exactly where to drop the hook for any given amount of scope.

In Figure 22-11, we see the drill. You should move slowly up to the drop point (usually heading into the wind) so that you can stop easily when you get there.

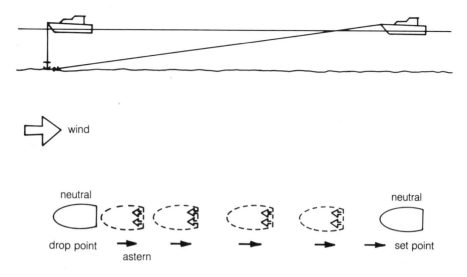

Figure 22-11

wind

neutral

drop point   astern   set point

neutral

THE ANCHORING DRILL   *Premeasure your desired scope and secure the rode to the cleat or post at that point. Loosely coil the rode you're going to pay out, taking care to arrange it so it won't snag or tangle. Then, after lowering the anchor at the desired drop point, simply back slowly until the rode becomes taut. If the rode remains slack when you've paid it all out, the anchor isn't set. Haul it in and start over!*

When you're ready to set the anchor, lower it (there's no need to throw it) until it touches bottom. Next, pay out the rode as you slowly back away, continuing until you have paid out the length you need, and then belay the rode on deck. When the anchor sets, you'll stop backing even with an engine in reverse at idle speed. If the rode gets taut, you'll know the anchor is set. If it vibrates (a result of the anchor bouncing along the bottom) and does not quickly become taut, haul in the anchor, go back to your drop point, and try again.

Incidentally, while 7:1 is a generally accepted scope, you'll set the anchor better and faster if you use more initially. Remember, the more nearly horizontal the pull, the better the penetration. You can shorten up to your desired swinging scope after the anchor is set. And if you are in a lunch-hook situation, you can (and often will) swing on shorter scope than 7:1. If the anchor is well set, the shorter scope shouldn't bother as long as you keep an eye out for possible dragging. Take bearings on objects ashore using a hand-bearing compass or the ship's compass. As long as they stay the same, you are in the same place, but if the bearings change appreciably, you have dragged and should let out more scope or move and reset the anchor.

How do you know how much rode you have out? You can guess, of course, but if you mark the rode every 5 or 10 feet (or in 6-foot—i.e., one-fathom—intervals), you won't have to. Chain links and braided nylon can be painted, and you can get numbered vinyl tabs to insert into twisted nylon. Marking the rode is well worth the time and effort.

One more word on scope. Though I've suggested that 70 feet of rode in 10 feet of water gives you a 7:1 scope, that's not quite true. It would be if you belayed the rode at the waterline, but since it will be belayed a few feet higher, the above-waterline distance should be considered also. If your foredeck cleat is 2 feet above the waterline and the water is 10 feet deep, you'll need to put out 84 feet of rode (7 X 12) to ensure a 7:1 scope.

Weighing Anchor

When it comes time to get the anchor out of the bottom and back aboard, you can usually use the same principle that helped you set it—only in reverse. If near horizontal pull makes the anchor penetrate and hold, vertical pull will break it free. Go ahead slowly, taking in slack, until the rode is vertical (Figure 22-12). Secure the rode at that point, power ahead a moment, and the anchor should break loose. Then all you have to do is haul it back aboard.

This technique will work in mud, clay, or sand. If rocks are involved, you'll more likely want to pull the anchor out just the opposite of the way it went in.

Figure 22-12

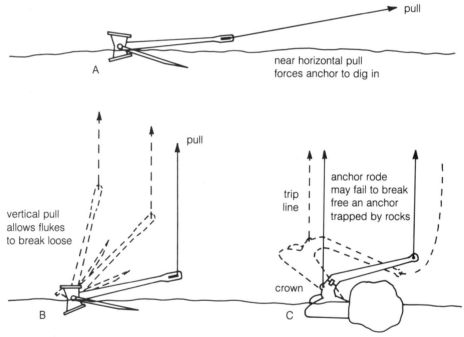

ANCHORS AWEIGH *Near horizontal pull makes an anchor hold; vertical pull will break it loose from mud, clay, or and. Shorten scope until the rode is straight up and down, secure it, apply a little power, and it should break free easily. When anchoring among rocks, you might wish to attach a trip line and float to the crown. Then, if the flukes become wedged under a rock and you cannot free the anchor with the rode, you have only to haul in the trip line and the anchor should come with it.*

One way to do this is to attach a trip line to the crown (Figure 22-12). To pull the anchor up, leave slack in the rode and haul in on the trip line.

It's also possible to use the rode to pull an anchor out backwards. As I mentioned, some lunch hooks are rigged to do this automatically. The shank is slotted (Figure 22-13) so that as long as the pull is basically horizontal, the rode stays at the end of the shank, but when the pull approaches vertical, the rode slides down toward the crown to pull the other way. Voila! The anchor comes loose. Figure 22-14 shows a way to rig any anchor to achieve the same effect. Attach the rode to the crown, then bring it up alongside the shank. Wrap a few turns of moderately heavy twine around the rode and shank, and the anchor will set and hold as long as the pull is basically horizontal. Shorten scope so the pull approaches vertical,

Figure 22-13

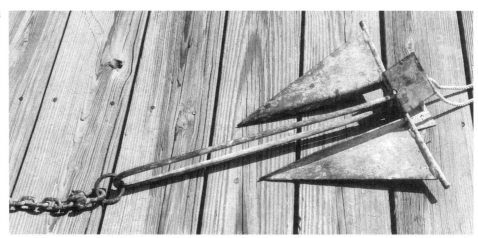

THE SLOTTED SHANK ANCHOR *Even in soft bottoms, pulling the anchor out by the crown is often the easiest way to recover it. Slotted-shank anchors aren't meant for unattended use, but work nicely as lunch hooks. As long as the pull is horizontal, the anchor holds. Bring the pull to vertical, however, and the rode slides toward the crown for easy retrieval.*

Figure 22-14

HOMEMADE QUICK RELEASE   *Secure the rode to the crown with a shackle and add a secondary connection to the shank with twine. A vertical pull will break the twine and move the application of force to the crown for easy extraction.*

and the twine will break, allowing the anchor to be pulled free easily. You may have to experiment with the size and amount of twine it takes to work with your particular boat and anchor, but with the right combination, it *will* work.

Comfort in Pairs

Though a single anchor will work nicely in the majority of anchoring situations, at times you need to set two. Say, for example, you are anchored in a narrow spot where there isn't enough room to swing on a change of tide (Figure 22-15).

The simplest solution is to set an anchor astern in addition to the one off the bow. The technique is easy. Set the bow anchor in normal fashion, then pay out about twice as much rode as you'll finally use. Drop back the extra rode as far as you can, then lower your spare anchor over the stern. Go ahead again and pay out the stern rode, taking in the bow rode until you are about in place (Figure 22-16). Make the stern rode fast to a stern cleat, leave the boat in gear for a moment to set the stern anchor, and there you are.

With this arrangement, you absolutely will not swing. This can be a plus, but it can also be a minus. If other boats in the anchorage are able to swing, you'll discover that not all things that go bump in the night are imaginary! You may also find that should the wind kick up astern, you'll take boarding seas at the point of lowest freeboard.

It's far better to be able to swing with the wind and tide but on a limited basis. The solution is the so-called Bahamian moor (Figure 22-17). The procedure is similar to that for setting bow and stern anchors, but after the second anchor is

Figure 22-15

Figure 22-16

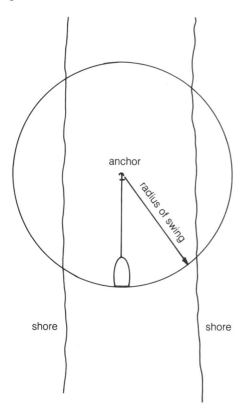

anchor

radius of swing

shore

shore

bow
anchor

shore

shore

stern
anchor

NO ROOM TO SWING *Whether the restriction is a nearby shoreline or other moored boats, you'll encounter occasions when the scope you need for proper holding creates a bigger swinging circle than you can realistically use.*

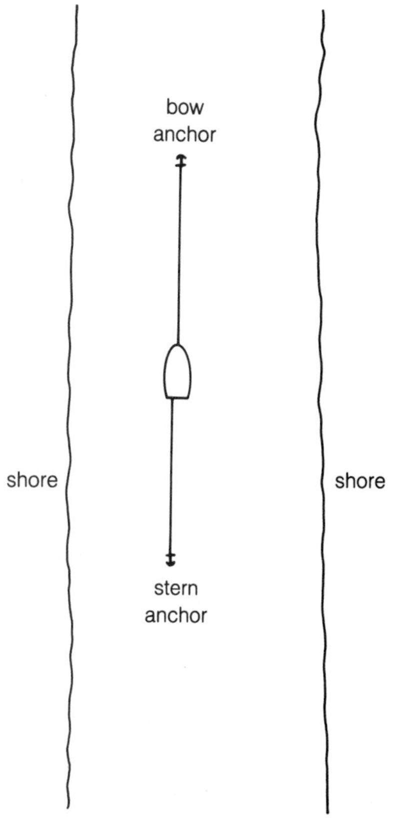

DUAL ANCHORS: BOW AND STERN *Setting anchors ahead and astern can keep you securely anchored with enough scope and no swing. Beware of other boats that can swing!*

set astern, its rode is led forward to belay. Your swing is limited, you have a secure anchor for each side of your swing (often better than relying on a single anchor to reset itself), but your bow will always point into prevailing weather.

Sometimes you need two anchors just for holding power. Say, for instance, you need to ride out a storm. Sheltering behind protective land is a possible solution to handling rough weather (Chapter 24), but although you *could* do this without anchoring, you'd have to resort to constant maneuvering to stay in place. You could lie to one anchor, but if the blow were strong enough, you might drag. After all, anchor selection is based on normal conditions. If you use two anchors, however, you can be reasonably sure of holding.

Figure 22-18 gives us the picture. If you set an anchor somewhere between 30 and 45 degrees to either side of the line of approach of the strongest winds and

Figure 22-17

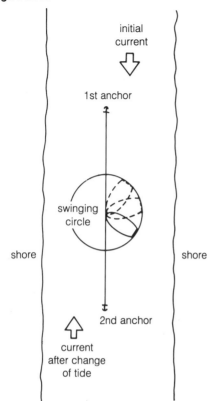

initial
current

1st anchor

swinging
circle

shore

shore

2nd anchor

current
after change
of tide

THE BAHAMIAN MOOR   *Setting two anchors 180 degrees apart but with both rodes brought to the bow lets you swing in a very restricted circle.*

Figure 22-18

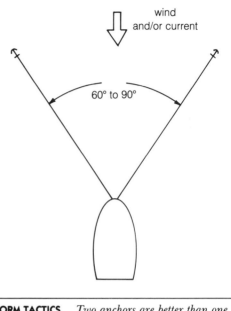

wind
and/or current

60° to 90°

STORM TACTICS   *Two anchors are better than one when extra holding is needed. Set them 60 to 90 degrees apart.*

seas, you will get maximum benefit from both anchors. Be sure to set each anchor securely with a direct pull and then use maximum scope.

While it is possible for one person to handle both the boat and the anchor, realistically anchoring is a two-"man" job. If you have the benefit of pulpit and windlass, anyone can handle the anchor end. If more physical strength is involved, many boating couples find that it is easier for the man to handle the anchor and rode while the woman handles the throttle(s) and clutch(es). However you do it, you'll find the drill goes more smoothly if you develop teamwork. A set of hand signals for come ahead, go back, stop, haul, lower, secure, etc., makes the process easier and eliminates a lot of shouting. It doesn't matter what the signals are as long as both teammates understand them. Make up your own. That can be a part of the fun.

23·Inlet Running

Inlet running, like most boathandling skills, is best learned by experience built up gradually over time—a luxury seldom granted those of us who don't encounter barred inlets in our boating backyards. All is not lost, however, and there is a quick way to gain "gradual" experience in running inlets at any stage of your boating career. First, let's examine the difficulties. As with other skills, running inlets begins with an understanding of what we have to overcome and why.

The Problems

The difficulties encountered at the mouth of a river or creek (or sometimes at a break in a barrier island), actually begin far at sea in wind-generated waves. The stronger the wind, the bigger the waves. If the wind blows from the same direction for an extended period of time or has the opportunity to blow unimpeded over a great distance, or *fetch,* the waves get even bigger.

Ocean waves generally resemble sine waves (Figure 23-1, A and B), though in real life they are more confused because several individual waves will traverse a given spot at the same time. The result is a complex wave, similar to a complex sound wave, in which individual waveforms combine to reinforce or cancel each other. This pattern of reinforcement leads to the observation that "every fifth (or third or seventh) wave is bigger." As long as the water depth exceeds one-half the wave length, the seas maintain a smooth form and are, except in severe storm conditions, no real threat.

Figure 23-1

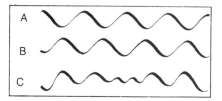

WAVEFORM *Individual ocean waves are essentially simple sine waves. However, the seas we encounter in boating are complex waves that result from the interaction of two or more simple wave systems of differing wave length. The combination produces irregular, but often predictable, patterns of smaller and larger seas.*

The problem develops when ocean waves move into shallower water (Figure 23-2). When a wave begins to "feel" the seabed, its sinusoidal movement is restricted, and the wave slows, permitting the next wave behind it to catch up. The top portion of the wave is less affected and thus tends to overrun the bottom portion, and the result is steeper, sharper, more closely spaced peaks, and eventually, as the seabed continues to shoal, the familiar curl of a wave approaching the beach. Forward motion and gravity combine to bring the curl downward, forming a breaker. A series of breakers is called surf.

The second element of the problem starts with the sand and silt brought downstream by outflowing current (Figure 23-3). The amount of suspended solids a given current can carry is directly related to its velocity. When an outflowing stream encounters the incoming surf, it slows and deposits some of the silt

Figure 23-2

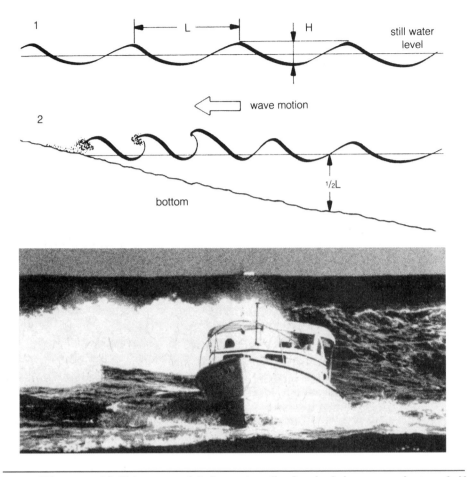

SURF *When waves "feel" the ocean or lake bottom (usually when depth decreases to about one-half the wave length), the result is steeper, sharper seas, and eventually cresting breakers, or surf.*

across the mouth of the inlet to form a sandbar. When the bar develops sufficiently, it changes the course of the stream, which in turn changes the development of the bar. Thus, inlets are in a constant state of change. A major ocean storm or runoff after a heavy inland rain can produce a big change in a hurry. Even in calm weather, change is constant and inevitable.

This presents several problems to boatmen. For instance, the meandering course of the outflow can eventually produce a channel that runs parallel to the breakers in the incoming surf. Fortunately, these stretches are often short, but even a few minutes of beam seas in heavy weather can be both uncomfortable and dangerous. Another problem is that buoys must be constantly moved to mark the best water. Thus, it is impossible to chart their location, and a cruising boatman has no way to preview the course through an inlet by studying the chart.

Figure 23-3

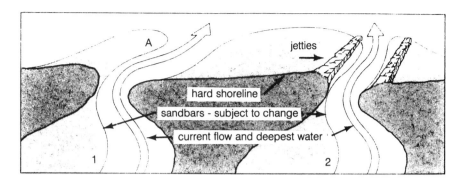

THE DEVELOPMENT OF AN INLET   *A typical natural inlet is shown in (1). Eventually silt will deposit to the right of point A and the current will either continue farther down the beach or perhaps break through the bar to the left of A. (2) The same inlet "improved." The jetties will help stabilize the inlet, but frequent dredging will be required to maintain the channel depth and remove the bars that will tend to form along the jetties.*

Man's Improvements?

Though constant change is the nature of the beast where inlets are concerned, we humans often can't resist trying to stop it. As a result, we have "improved" many inlets by adding breakwaters or jetties and by dredging and redredging the channel to make it go where we want it to. The truth is that while these man-made changes can slow down nature's changes, they can't eliminate them. Even improved inlets change, though the change is often slowed enough to render them more predictable and easier to run.

Strategy and Tactics

The most practical way to learn inlet running is to go ahead and do it. But begin gently. For your first attempt, pick a time when you have an offshore wind and slack water, or the early stages of a rising tide. Starting with an improved inlet helps. If you can't get ideal conditions, two out of three isn't bad, but be sure to avoid onshore winds in your initial attempts. Even under the best conditions a problem inlet should have enough surge to give you a good indication of what you must work with (and against) and of what to expect under worse conditions.

If you are starting on an unimproved or natural inlet, be sure to go out through it before trying to come in. This will give you a better picture of the sandbar and surf patterns. In fact, this brings up one of the biggest dangers in inlet running: From the outside it is very hard to determine the state of the seas, since the backs of waves all look very much alike; the clues to roughness are mostly on the inside. With practice, you will note subtle indicators visible from the outside, but this degree of observational skill takes time to develop.

Beginning with the easy surge of ideal conditions, practice the proper techniques until they feel natural. If the surge is very gentle, technique won't really matter, but take advantage of the opportunity to get used to feeling the rhythm

Figure 23-4

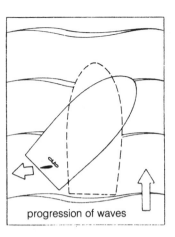

progression of waves

STAYING SQUARE   *The first secret to safe inlet running is to stay square to the seas. While* staying *square is often impossible, the trick is to get squared away again quickly before the next sea can kick you.*

of the sea. Next, try the inlet on an outgoing tide with all other conditions ideal. You'll notice a difference. When you have mastered that, move on to gentle onshore winds. Ultimately, you'll be ready to face the worst conditions: an outgoing tide against a strong onshore wind.

Throughout your practice sessions, your objective is to maintain control. Just how you do that depends greatly on your boat and how she handles. If you have twin screws and a lot of power, often you can just pour on the coal and outrun, or at least ride *with*, the seas. If you try to use speed alone, be sure you can go fast enough to skip across the crests or stay with one. Remember, shallowness is one of the problems presented by inlets. This is accentuated in the troughs. More than one speedster has torn off underwater running gear and holed a boat by coming off the crest of a wave and down into so little water that the boat momentarily grounded—hard! So if you opt for the fast lane, do so with care.

A more cautious approach is to enter the inlet on the back of a wave, neither too close to the curl nor too close to the wave behind (Figure 23-5). This is easier said than done, but you can learn with practice; developing the proper pacing is one of the reasons for practicing under gradually worsening conditions. Entering on the back of a wave is step one; adjusting your speed to stay there is step two (and in my opinion, a wiser choice than barreling onward, even if you have the power). If you don't have the power to keep up with the wave system, you'll have to learn to use the power you do have with finesse and let the waves outrun you without upsetting you.

If the seas are overtaking you, try to keep your stern square to the waves so that there will be less tendency for the boat to swing sideways—a move known as "broaching." You should avoid this because heavy beam seas can lead to capsizing if their frequency should happen to coincide with the rolling moment of your boat. Repeated beam seas, like the repeated gentle pushes of a child on a swing,

Figure 23-5

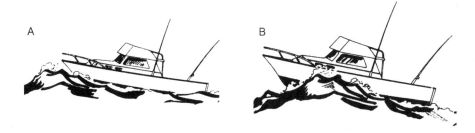

A   B

WAVE-BACK RIDING   *The second secret of inlet running is to try to stay on the back of a wave near the crest (A). Getting ahead of the crest (B) can lead to either dropping into the shallows or surfing out of control. Dropping too far behind the crest may leave you in dangerously shallow water and invite the wave behind to come crashing down into your cockpit.*

A boat that lacks the power to either outrun or even keep up with the waves must let them pass. The toughest moments come when the crest of the overtaking wave passes beneath you.

can accomplish more in total effect than a large, strong single wave. Staying squared away has to be a prime objective.

Square It Up

At times the sea will win out and swing you around. When it does, take corrective action immediately. Back off on the throttle(s) and turn the steering wheel to swing the bow in the direction you want to go. Then give a burst of forward power. The purpose of this operation is to swing the boat back stern to the seas, so you'll have to ease off on the throttle(s) and straighten out the rudders as soon as you near the desired heading or you'll overcompensate and swing the other way. You have to act fast, because you want to be squared away before the next wave can catch you abeam. This sort of throttle and steering-wheel game can go on repeatedly until you reach calmer water. It's work, but it will get you through some really rough inlets unscathed.

Pitchpoling, or turning end over end, is another possibility one faces when running a treacherous inlet. Pitchpoling occurs when the bow buries itself in the wave ahead while the wave behind lifts the aft section up and over. It *can* happen, though the shape, relative lightness, and shallow draft of most powerboats make it more of a theoretical problem than a practical one. It would be most apt to happen after a wild, out-of-control ride on the curl of a wave followed by a slide down the steep front face (surfing, if you will). While pitchpoling is less likely than broaching, its mere possibility is another good reason for trying to stay on the back of a wave. Here's another. Remember, you only have control when your prop(s) and rudder(s) are in the water. Get too far up onto the top of a wave, and it will lift your after section out of the water. And that can lead to trouble. On the other hand, staying too far back leaves you open to being "pooped"—a calamity in which the wave behind breaks and comes crashing down on you. This presents two not-so-pleasant possibilities. Having a wave's worth of water coming down on you can do considerable damage in its own right, and worse, since the trough is the thinnest water you'll encounter, being pooped can cause the same kind of grounding damage to a slow boat that flying off a crest can do to a fast one.

As I said, keeping a boat constantly squared to the seas and on the back of a wave (if possible) requires nearly constant work with the throttle(s) and steering wheel. And work is the operative word. In fact, a trip through a rough inlet can be downright exhausting. But the results are worth it.

Final Caveats

No matter how adept you become at running inlets, never lose your respect for the power of the sea. A treacherous inlet can be difficult (and sometimes dangerous) even for the experienced. Size up every situation before entering to make sure that both you and your boat are up to it. When in doubt, stay out.

———————◆———————

24. How to Handle Heavy Weather

The best way to handle heavy weather is to avoid it—as much as you possibly can! And I don't mean that facetiously. Too many people find themselves in uncomfortable seas simply because they fail to pay attention to the weather. With NOAA radio stations now broadcasting in nearly every boating region and with inexpensive weather receivers available at Radio Shack stores, there's no excuse for the skipper of even the smallest boat not knowing what major weather activity is forecast. Beyond that, you should work on developing a good weather eye (along with all your other seaman's tricks). The indicators are many and too varied by regional and seasonal influences to go into here, but the old-timers in your area will undoubtedly know them well. Cultivate friendships among other boatmen (which should be easy, because boatmen are usually the friendly sort) and pick their brains. Soon you'll be recognizing the signs by yourself. Typically, particular changes in wind direction, certain cloud formations, and specific combinations of wind direction and cloud type will be the forerunners of bad weather. Nature can be very predictable—at least in the short term.

Weather Signs

I remember from my early childhood that I *knew* it was about to rain whenever I could hear carousel music at our home. The amusement park at the beach was over a mile away, and we hardly ever heard a sound from it. But when that music came wafting in, the rain soon followed. I thought it was magic! When I got older, my father explained the reason: Whenever our summer wind backed around from its usual southwesterly flow to come out of the east, it was a sign of impending bad weather—an approaching low-pressure system. Since we lived west of the amusement park, we could only hear the merry-go-round at our house when there was wind out of the east. It wasn't magic, but it was a reliable omen. Various sights, sounds, and smells can all work the same way to tip you off to changes that portend trouble. All you have to do is learn what they are for your boating area, and keep that weather eye peeled. It doesn't do much good to know the signs if you are too "busy" to look for them.

When the Going Gets Rough

One of the corollaries to Murphy's famous law ("Anything that can go wrong will go wrong") is that despite your best efforts to avoid it, bad weather will sneak up on you sometime during your boating career, and when you least expect it. Since it is this sneaky kind of heavy weather that we most often encounter in small pleasureboats, we'll forego discussion of mid-ocean gales, tropical storms, and other such extreme conditions and concentrate rather on what to do when we get surprised by sudden storms in inland and coastal boating areas.

Some of the nastiest chop I've ever encountered was on so-called protected waters. Just as the seas can be challenging in inlets, small, shallow bodies of water can get nasty *because* they are shallow. When a strong wind kicks up, the water doesn't have the depth to accommodate the long, gentle swells encountered offshore. Instead, we get short, steep, and often very confused seas.

Chapter 1 suggested that a fair-weather boat on inland waters need not be as seaworthy as a craft intended for serious ocean-tournament fishing. I'll stand by that advice. In this context it means that you will probably have a more lightly built boat for sheltered waters than if you had planned to go offshore, and that means comparable seas are going to toss you around more than they would a heavier craft.

Yet, since boats as a whole can usually take much more punishment than their occupants, this is often more a matter of comfort than safety. Properly handled, that small, light boat you never expected to have out in the bad stuff will keep you safe indeed. The key, of course, lies in the phrase "properly handled."

Examine Your Options

Your exact approach to heavy-weather boathandling depends a lot on your boat, of course. It also depends on where you are, where the bad weather is when you first realize it's coming your way, how bad it's going to be when it gets to you, and how fast it's coming. There's no simple panacea that will work every time. Let's examine a few strategies.

Run Away

Even if you can't avoid bad weather entirely, you may be able to escape the worst of it by outrunning the storm. If you have a fast boat, there's a distinct possibility that you can move *much* faster than the weather. Using your potential speed to get away from heavy seas is often your wisest choice.

Where do you go? Home is the best bet if you can get there safely. Even if heading home will take you toward the storm, it can still be a good idea *if* you have the speed to get there and get your boat secured *before* the storm hits. On the other hand, you absolutely do not want to be caught by high winds and choppy seas just as you're coming in. Adding storm conditions to the other elements of close-quarters maneuvering is begging disaster. Never run toward a storm unless you are absolutely certain you can beat it to your destination.

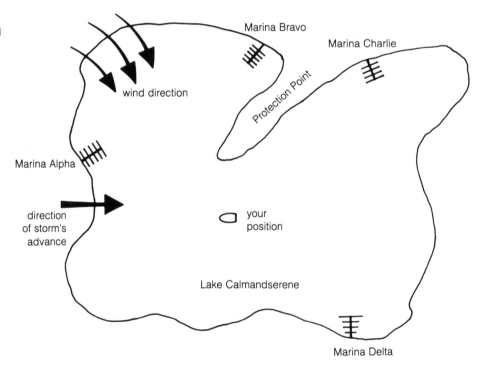

Figure 24-1

Marina Bravo

Marina Charlie

wind direction

Protection Point

Marina Alpha

direction of storm's advance

your position

Lake Calmandserene

Marina Delta

ESCAPING ROUGH WEATHER *If "home" is Marina Alpha, Charlie, or Delta, you might be able to get there before the storm. Head for Alpha only if you are quite sure you have enough time. If home is Marina Bravo, consider other options—it is not as close as Alpha or Delta, doesn't offer the potential protection of Charlie, and would expose you to a lee shore that could be dangerous if the storm arrived before you made it home. Delta is closer than Charlie but will probably be rougher when the storm hits. Charlie will probably be calmer, but will take longer to reach and will put you farther from home.*

Find a Harbor of Refuge

If getting home safely is questionable, perhaps there is a closer port, or one that lies in a direction away from the storm. It should offer the opportunity either to escape the bad weather entirely (not always a sure thing under any circumstances) or to properly secure the boat before the bad weather hits. You'll need a marina with available slip space or an anchorage area with good holding ground, and some kind of shelter ashore would certainly be desirable. (After all, why not try to get *completely* away from the weather by going ashore for awhile?) The most important attribute of your harbor of refuge, however, is that you should be able to get there in time to beat the weather.

Hide

Even if you can't make port in time to avoid the storm, you might be able to escape the brunt of it by sheltering behind an island or some other protective piece of land. Generally speaking, the seas in the lee of a point or island will be considerably calmer than those receiving the full force of the wind. Check your charts. If limited protection is available and you can reach it quickly, it can often be safer and more comfortable than "better" shelter you can't reach before the storm does. Be sure the waters are bold, with adequate depth right up under the land and few if any ledges lurking.

Dodge the Storm

Lacking radar, weather instruments, and other gear that operators of large craft may have to help define a storm's boundaries, small-boat skippers have a poorer chance of taking this action effectively. Yet the old eyeball can help here, too, at

Figure 24-2

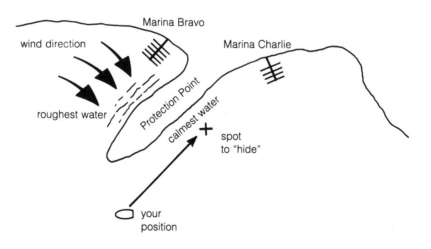

FINDING A HIDEOUT   *If you can't make it to a marina, find some protective land to hide behind. You can anchor or just sit and wait, depending on how long you expect the bad weather to last.*

least to a degree. The center of a storm is usually darker and denser, while the edges fade to a whiter shade of pale. Using such hints as a guide, you can often work your way to the edges of and eventually completely away from a storm. This tactic carries no guarantee, but if begun soon enough, it can work. It's often worth the try.

Riding It Out

If you can't avoid a storm and are forced to ride it out, you can take a number of actions to make a bad situation better. Probably the first is to find deeper water. Though you may think staying close to land is your best bet, this simply isn't true. Deeper water will usually be calmer because the waves have room to develop a smoother, gentler form. Heading away from shore is, many times, the path to a more comfortable ride.

You particularly want to avoid a lee shore. When you get too close to the shore the wind is blowing onto, you not only risk the danger of being driven ashore should you lose propulsion power, you also face the worst waters in the storm sector.

Here's the problem. As the storm seas approach shore, they encounter shallower and shallower water, which creates a steeper and steeper chop. Then, as the waves crash against the shore and rebound, they generate conflicting seas from the opposite direction. Add the fact that the shore is rarely a straight line so that rebounding seas can come back from several directions, and you have confusion of the first order. Stay well away from any shore that doesn't offer protection.

In summary: If the shoreline is between you and the direction from which the wind is blowing, that's good. You have at the very least a degree of shelter. If you

Figure 24-3

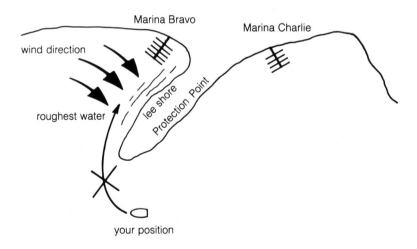

AVOIDING TROUBLE   *Don't put yourself between the weather and a lee shore. The water will be rougher there, and engine failure could put you on the beach. In this instance, running for Marina Bravo would be a bad idea.*

are between the wind and the shore, that's bad. You're in the worst possible position, so get out of there fast, or as quickly as conditions allow. Which brings us to the next point. . . .

Adjust Your Speed to the Seas

Running away at full throttle is a practical option only before the bad weather hits. Once it's upon you, you must adopt a different strategy, and that inevitably calls for slowing down. Inexperienced skippers often make the mistake of slowing to a dead crawl. Sometimes this is your only choice, but more often you'll find that the most comfortable speed, while certainly slower than full throttle (or even normal cruise), is faster than flat idle. Look for a balance between the pounding you get from going too fast and the bobbing-cork, limited-control feeling you get from going too slow. Remember, rudder action is largely dependent on a good flow of discharge screw current across it. If you slow down too much, steering suffers. On the other hand, going too fast can be not only uncomfortable but counterproductive—you also lose control if your props come out of the water! Experiment a bit, and you should be able to find the optimum speed for the conditions you're facing.

Please note, however, that in many seas there won't *be* a comfortable speed. To maintain both control and comfort, you'll have to adjust the throttle constantly, much as you would in running an inlet.

Take the Seas at the Proper Angle

Most of the time, this means slightly off the bow, although sometimes it can be comfortable to take the seas on the quarter (that is, on the corner of the transom). As much as possible, avoid taking seas either directly on the bow or against the transom. Avoid beam seas no matter what.

Since taking the seas at an angle more or less dictates the direction in which you must proceed, you'll often have to zigzag toward a destination—particularly if that destination lies in the direction from which the storm is blowing. The easiest method is to take a given number of waves on one side—say on the port bow—then swing and take the same number on the starboard. This will allow you to make good a course over the ground (straight into the storm) that would be uncomfortable or even unsafe if pursued directly into the teeth of the wind and seas.

Many of the principles of inlet running apply here. You don't want to broach, you need to maintain control, you don't want to surf or be pooped, and you want to keep props and rudders in the water and working. In short, you're probably going to have to do some work with both steering and throttle(s) to maintain the boat's most comfortable attitude, which is, as in inlet running, close to but slightly behind the crest of any wave you are riding.

Another way of putting it is: *Try to stay on the "high ground."* Just as you might smooth out a ride down a rough dirt road by steering around potholes, you can often smooth out rough seas by following a wave train from crest to crest. Though each is to some degree an individual entity, waves tend to run in groups. You can't see it when you're in a trough, but when you are high on the back of

Figure 24-4

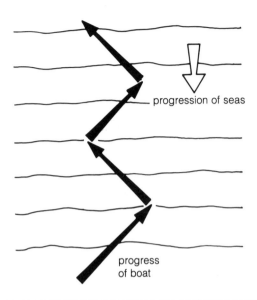

progression of seas

progress
of boat

ZIGZAGGING   *In steep seas, a straight line is the roughest distance between two points. Taking the seas on alternate sides of the bow may make the trip take longer, but the ride will be smoother.*

a wave you can often discern a bridging pattern between adjacent crests of even the most confused seas. If you try to follow that pattern (and *try* is the best you can do; the "high ground" at sea doesn't hold still as it does ashore), you will usually have a smoother ride than if you ignore the pattern and slide repeatedly back down into a trough. Staying up offers another advantage: You can see better, which is a practical and psychological plus. In both respects, it beats looking at the walls of water that are all you can see when you're in a trough.

Heave To

Sometimes, making headway, even with the slightest progress, is just too much for comfort. In that case you should try to sit still until the storm blows over. You still may need to work with the steering wheel and throttle(s), but your objective now is merely to help the boat hold its most comfortable attitude to the seas. This can call for an occasional burst of power to nudge the bow around, but before you get carried away, see how the boat rides when you take a hands-off approach. You could discover that the boat and nature work well together; the boat may lie stern to the seas, which is fine as long as the waves are not short and steep enough to break over the transom. Just be ready to take corrective action if the boat wants to lie with the seas abeam. Chances are, it won't, and you'll find that the boat drifts with the weather more comfortably than when you try to fight it. Of course you have to keep an eye out to make sure you don't drift into danger and be ready to apply power at any time if corrective action is called for.

   If you have to heave to, it usually won't be for long—maybe just through the very worst of the storm. In fact, the upside of all this (yes, even bad weather has an upside) is that the kind of storm that develops so quickly that it sneaks up on you most often blows over just as quickly—long-lasting bad weather usually provides better advance warning. No matter how rough the water gets, you can take heart in the thought that it should soon calm down.

General Precautions

Whatever actions you take to minimize the effects of nature's nastiness, there are other actions that should accompany them. I've saved them for last because they are probably the *most important* elements of heavy-weather boathandling and apply universally.

Act Quickly

As I've already said, avoiding bad weather is still the best thing you can do, and that entails reacting quickly to the warning signs. Even when it's too late to avoid bad weather completely, however, you shouldn't delay making your move to run, hide, or find the best of the worst. This advice applies particularly to the next two items.

Secure Anything Loose

If your boat is going to start bouncing around, you don't want things within it bouncing too. Naturally, it's easier to secure loose gear while you still have a relatively stable platform—hence the advice to act quickly. Anything you can't get lashed before it gets rough may have to remain on the loose until the weather calms down again. Depending on what they are and where they are, such objects can range from mere mess makers to potentially destructive missiles.

Wear PFDs

This is an unpleasant prospect for some people, who equate the wearing of personal flotation devices (PFDs, or life jackets) with impending disaster. Actually, to wear a flotation device is only to recognize a simple fact: if you are aboard a small, bouncing boat, you have at least a possibility of making a misstep that could put you overboard. The odds are great that it won't happen, but it can. Be prepared for the possibility no matter how remote it may seem.

One of the easiest ways to get others to wear their PFDs (without resorting to issuing an order) is for the skipper to don his or hers first. Leading by example is often best. As the captain, you are responsible for everyone aboard. If all else fails, insist! Make sure there are no exceptions.

Stay Put

One way people aboard can increase their odds against falling overboard is to find a seat and stay in it. If you aren't moving about, you can't make a misstep. It's that simple. This, too, may call for an order, although it's usually easier to get people to sit than to wear a PFD.

That's really all there is to it. The worst part is that the first couple of times you get caught in heavy weather, you will be doing things from scratch. Advice and suggestions are fine, but you can't beat having been there. You can, however, get your basic skills well under control. If you do that, the rough stuff will be much easier to handle.

———————◆———————

25. Practice Makes Perfect

While I've tried to make the learning process easier by providing basic knowledge to build upon, you can only complete your education by getting out there and putting it into practice. And practice is the operative word: learning through repetition. If you think I'm suggesting that you buy a boat to have a good time and then turn it into nothing but work, think again. Boats are meant to be fun, and this part should be no exception. If you handle it right, the learning can be fully as enjoyable as any other boating activity. The bonus is that by quickly (relatively speaking) getting to know your boat better, and becoming a better boathandler, you make the other activities more fun than they ever could be otherwise.

Take docking for instance (see Chapter 16). It can be traumatic. Crowded marina, minimal maneuvering room, tight berth, people watching, inexperienced skipper and crew—these are definitely the elements of disaster and pain. But if you add the knowledge gained through experience, you can perform magic, transforming this horror show to a veritable symphony of deft maneuvers. If the only docking practice you get is that which comes without choice in the course of your other boating activities, you'll remain inexperienced for a long, long time.

The answer is to make practice fun in itself by setting up practice days as special boating events. Want to become more proficient at docking? Then create a practice pier. Buy a piece of Styrofoam to use as a float, a couple of small anchors to hold it in place ("fisherman's mushrooms," those 10-pound mushroom anchors, will do), and enough line to secure the float to the anchors. Take your practice float to a quiet area where you won't be disturbed by other boats, nosy spectators, or other distractions, and set it in place. Then start practicing. Come in for landing after landing after landing, and critique yourself each time. The Styrofoam won't damage your topsides if you come in too hard, and being out there away from everyone else should prevent your mistakes from damaging your pride.

When you get to be pretty good at handling the conditions at the chosen location, find a different one that will offer greater or different challenges. Or, lacking another location, at least raise one anchor and swing the float so it presents a different face to the prevailing conditions. Then try again. And again.

Don't Forget Your Crew

You should make an effort to remember (because it can be so easy to overlook) that the learning experience should extend to everyone who will normally be boating with you. Amateur captains often envy us professionals because we have an equally professional crew to help us. Well, we often do. However, *more* often we have only slightly experienced beginning professionals. After we spend a lot of time and effort training them, they move on to a better job (such as a novice captain), and we start training again. As a pleasureboat skipper, you can have the advantage of a reasonably permanent crew—your family—if you play your cards right. The essentials are: getting them involved, keeping them involved, and treating them with respect and kindness through it all. Always remember that they are beginners, too. That's why it's important to have them practice with you. Whatever the maneuver, assign everyone a job, explain what you want done, and then let them learn to do it with you.

I had to learn this lesson the hard way, from a boating companion many years ago. She was a very attractive and bright young lady who enjoyed boating as much as I did and was a delight to have aboard. But she had not been involved with boats as long as I had, and we had just begun cruising together. Consequently, she didn't always do what I thought was right and I let her know it in no uncertain terms. One evening as we watched a large British motoryacht being put through a rather tricky maneuver with near effortless precision, I couldn't resist commenting.

"Did you notice how efficiently each crewmember performed?" I asked, with an expression that made it obvious I expected the same efficiency aboard my boat.

"Yes, I did," she replied with a bigger smile than I thought appropriate. "And did *you* notice," she continued as her smile grew even broader, "that the captain never yelled at them once?"

Ouch! She was right. You shouldn't yell at your crew unless they are in immediate danger and you want them to move quickly out of harm's way. In any other situation, you'll get better cooperation by staying calm. A yelling skipper is an insecure skipper who does *not* have the sort of control of the situation we all think a person in command should have. No matter how much experience you have, there will be times you'll feel out of control. "The secret of professionalism," a very talented Downeaster I worked with once told me, "is knowing how to correct the situation when things go wrong. Anyone can learn to do the job when there isn't a problem, but a professional will make it come out right even when there is." He was right. And the better you feel about the situation, the more competently you'll think and act. Practice helps.

Here's another way to avoid the need for yelling: Make sure all your crewmembers know what you expect them to do *before* you need to have it done. Then all it takes is a nod or a hand signal meaning "now," and they'll know it's time to do it. When you are prepared and they are prepared (as you will be if you practice together), you and your family can look just as sharp as any white-uniformed professional crew.

Take It Slow and Easy

Training experts tell us that learning takes place on a curve. Whether we're trying to shape up our bodies or our minds, the first few repetitions don't do much. Then we begin to see some gain. But if we work at it too long, the gain diminishes in proportion to the effort put forth. So don't overwork any single exercise. After you've practiced docking for a while, either quit and go play or try something else. Don't push to the point of boredom or diminishing returns. It's supposed to be fun, and it will be, as long as you keep a healthy attitude.

Practice well enough, and you'll be able to handle a boat like an old-time harbormaster I once knew in Maine. The man could make a boat do nearly anything; any watercraft he operated was like a marionette in the hands of a master puppeteer. One day I watched him back a single-screw lobsterboat into a tight slip as easily as most landlubbers could put a Volkswagon into a Cadillac's parking space. Someone else on the pier saw him, too, and commented, "Wow, you parked that boat just like a car!" The old-timer drew himself up proudly, looked his observer squarely in the eye, and announced, "I did not! I handled her like a boat."

———————◆———————

Appendix 1.
RULES OF THE ROAD

Before you head out on the water, you should be aware of the nautical Rules of the Road. These exist for one purpose: the prevention of collisions at sea. For this reason, the international rules are also known as the Collision Regulations, or COLREGS for short.

Prior to 1980, the United States had three sets of rules for inland waters alone (Inland Rules, Great Lakes Rules, and Western River Rules), in addition to those that applied in offshore waters. Fortunately, things are much simpler and more uniform now. The International Rules apply to "ocean waters" (which begin at the mouth of each inlet in most areas), and the Inland Rules apply everywhere else in the U.S. The two sets of rules are identically formatted and very similar, differing only in a few particulars. Both sets are contained in the Coast Guard publication, *Navigation Rules, International-Inland* (COMDTINST M16672.2A), available in most places where navigation charts are sold. I suggest you get a copy and study it well. A thorough knowledge of the Rules of the Road is so important that the Coast Guard demands a minimum score of 90% on the rules section of its captain's license exams, while 70 suffices for passing other portions.

When you first skim through your copy of COMDTINST M16672.2A (who comes up with these titles, anyway?) you'll be amazed at the extent and apparent complexity of its contents. But when you really dig in, you'll realize that while they are extensive, the COLREGS are not as complicated as they first appear. Indeed, when you consider only the basic *operating* rules (the "steering and sailing rules" as opposed to the rules regarding vessel lights, "day shapes" for special situations, and such), they are quite straightforward.

A friend once summed up the Rules of the Road in one simple statement: "Safety first and keep to the right." Perhaps this is an oversimplification, but it *is* the essence of what the rules are about.

So, without intending to suggest that you shouldn't also study the Coast Guard publication, I'd like to expand a bit on my friend's statement and cover the practical application of the rules in the hope that it will further your understanding of their intent.

Safety First

Though they make their points in formal terms, in many ways the rules merely ask for common sense. The requirement that "every vessel shall at all times maintain a proper lookout," for example, means simply that a skipper should always be watching where the boat is going and what's going on around it. If other related activities (such as checking your position on a chart or looking through a guide book for the location of a marina) cause you to take your eyes off the water for more than a second or two, you should have another pair of eyes do the watching until you can be your own "lookout" again. You should also engage the services of "extra eyes" whenever visibility worsens. Use of radar or an autopilot does not release you from the obligation of maintaining a visual lookout.

The rules also require that you "at all times proceed at a safe speed," and that in determining how fast is "safe" you take into consideration such important factors as visibility, sea and weather conditions, the handling characteristics of your boat, maneuvering room, potential hazards, and other vessel traffic.

Meeting Situation

In most **meeting** situations (you and another boat approaching each other head on or nearly head on), you should keep to the right. If the other vessel does the same, you'll go by port side to port side, just as we do on the highway. This precept holds particularly in narrow channels. If you are already so far to the left of the vessel you're meeting that "keeping to the right" would cause you to cross in front of it, stay to the left and meet starboard to starboard. *Most* of the time, however, you'll keep out of trouble by holding to the right side of a channel or waterway. (Here is one case where the Inland Rules go beyond the International Rules: The former hold that upstream of tidal waters, a vessel bound downstream has right of way over one heading upstream. The International Rules, for obvious reasons, need no rule to cover this situation.)

We'll discuss "right-of-way" rules shortly. In many cases, the question of who goes first can be puzzling to newcomers, yet the rules are explicit. By establishing a definitive order of who yields when, we seek to prevent the "after-you-no-after-you" confusion we sometimes experience in doorways ashore. What is at worst an embarrassing inconvenience ashore could lead to collision on the water, and as Thucydides said, a collision at sea can ruin your entire day. If everyone in command of a boat knows and follows the rules, there should be no confusion.

Crossing Situation

Since you will probably want a bit of experience under your belt before you begin running after dark, a discussion of navigation lights is probably premature at this point. However, the way lights are arranged relates directly to right of way, so it might help to consider the lights on your boat even if you don't plan to use them soon.

Figure A-1 shows the four basic "navigation" lights on a typical powerboat. The red sidelight is visible through an arc from dead ahead to 22.5 degrees abaft the port beam. The green sidelight covers a similar arc to starboard. The white masthead light covers the arc of both sidelights, while the white sternlight fills in the gap — the portion of the circle not covered by the others.

The area from straight ahead to 22.5 degrees abaft your starboard beam is generally called the "danger zone." It's no coincidence that this is the area covered by your green navigation light — skippers of boats within this arc have the right of way and can consider the green to mean go. Under the rules, you must give way to every vessel within this arc. In any **crossing** situation that could result in collision, these vessels would be showing you their red lights (which you can take to mean stop). Of course you don't absolutely have to *stop*. You can also

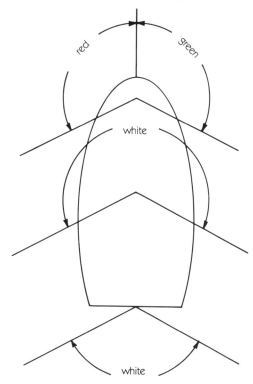

give way by slowing down or changing course (to the right, please) or by taking any combination of these actions. You can even keep going straight ahead at the same speed if you are absolutely certain you will pass well clear of the other vessel (as you would if she were going fast enough to pass ahead of you or you were going fast enough to pass ahead), but it isn't always wise to do so. Just remember, if you have a boat in your danger zone, it is incumbent upon *you* to avoid collision. The other boat is technically bound to *stand on* (maintain course and speed), while you are charged with the obligation to *give way.* If you have a collision, "I thought I had room to clear" won't cut it.

Pecking Order

While you must give way to *every* vessel in your danger zone, in other situations the matter of who gives way and when doesn't seem quite as clear-cut. But it is. For example, you must always give way to a vessel you are **overtaking,** whenever you approach within the arc described by the other vessel's sternlight. That doesn't mean you can't pass, it just means that until you are well ahead of the other boat, *you* are the one burdened with the responsibility of staying out of the way. (Though the current terms "stand-on" vessel and "give-way" vessel are clearer in some ways, the formerly used expressions of "privileged" and "burdened" had some coherent meaning, too.)

We have now covered the three "passing situations": meeting, crossing, and overtaking. "OK," you might ask, "but what about other situations? For instance, don't sailboats always have the right of way?" Good question. The answer is, most of the time, but not *always.* For example, if a fast multihull under sail overtakes a slow displacement trawler under power, the overtaking vessel is still the give-way vessel, regardless of its means of propulsion. And then, too, as far as the rules are concerned, an auxiliary sailboat becomes a powerboat if its engine is running, whether or not it also has sails up. And there are other instances in which sailboats must give way, as we shall now see.

As is often the case in life, there's a pecking order on the water. "New Reels Catch Fish, So Purchase Some" is a mnemonic to help remember it. From most privileged to least, the order is: *N*ot under command, *R*estricted in ability to maneuver; *C*onstrained by draft; *F*ishing boats; *S*ailboats; *P*owerboats; *S*ea-planes. Each category must give way to *all* those above it.

"Not under command" doesn't mean no one's in charge. Rather it refers to a vessel that has lost its steering or propulsion or both, and thus absolutely *cannot* maneuver — it is at everyone else's mercy.

You might think that the term "restricted in ability to maneuver" would mean the same thing. Under the rules, however, this refers to a vessel that is able to maneuver but only with difficulty because of the work it is doing at the time — the term covers dredges, buoy tenders, survey vessels, and such.

"Constrained by draft" refers to ships (or even large boats) that cannot leave the channel and go into shallower water and thus do not have the option of turning. Therefore, they only have to give way to vessels higher on the list, which have even fewer options.

"Fishing boats" means only the commercial variety, and only when they are dragging nets or trawls. Sportfishermen don't come under this banner, even when they are trolling, and neither do commercial fishing boats when they are not actually engaged in the act of fishing.

"Sailboats" as a category is clear-cut, but, as mentioned above, if they are under power they are powerboats under the rules.

The Law of Gross Tonnage

The common thread in all this is relative maneuverability. The intent of the rules is that the more maneuverable vessel must stay out of the way of the less maneuverable. Simple as that. So, while bigger vessels aren't given special consideration in the rules (other than in the constrained-by-draft category), practicality suggests that they should be given special consideration on the water. If you're zipping about in a 21-foot outboard-powered center console, you and that 110-foot steel sightseeing boat beside you are on equal grounds, legally speaking. But you have more maneuverability and carry less draft, so when push comes to shove (perhaps not the best phrase to use when talking about collision avoidance) you would be well advised to stay out of his way. This admonition takes on greater meaning when "the other guy" is even bigger, say a freighter or tanker. When you realize that a large ship underway at cruising speed needs a mile or more to stop or complete a turn, you can see why this is healthy advice. I hardly need point out who will come out second best if there *is* a collision.

In keeping with this theory of relative maneuverability, though I've made the point that sailboats under power are powerboats under the rules, keep in mind that your powerboat will still have greater maneuverability than most sailboats (particularly when the sailboat is larger). Act accordingly.

Timely Actions

I'd like to end this discussion of the Rules of the Road with a bit of advice that tempers the rules' stated operational requirements with some practical insight.

First, the rules require that the give-way vessel give way in such a manner that the stand-on vessel can clearly see your intentions. If you are changing course, make one big, *obvious* change rather than a series of slight and perhaps imperceptible changes. Likewise, if you are slowing down or stopping, make the action clearly visible. In short, comply with the rules' objective of removing ambiguity. Let the other skipper *know* you are giving way.

The rules require that the stand-on vessel maintain course and speed to avoid confusion, but, as I've suggested, there will be times when you should follow the more practical option of getting out of the way of a less maneuverable vessel even if you are, technically, the stand-on vessel. In this case, too, be sure your intentions are made clear to the skipper of the larger vessel soon enough to avoid confusion and potential problems.

Incidentally, taking such action is not as much a departure from the rules as you might think. Rule 17, the same one that tells you the stand-on vessel must maintain course and speed, also states that if it appears a give-way vessel isn't taking appropriate action, the stand-on vessel should do whatever is necessary to avoid collision. Since "The Law of Gross Tonnage" is involved only when common sense tells you it is necessary — that is, when the less maneuverable vessel cannot take proper action — your doing so actually follows the letter as well as the intent of the rules.

There's more to the Rules of the Road than we could cover here, of course; that's why you should study the Coast Guard book itself. But if you understand what I've outlined above, you are ready to go boating.

—————◆—————

Appendix 2.

A GALLERY OF
POWERBOATS

A great variety of powerboats ply North American waters. The photographs that follow scarcely scratch the surface, and are intended mainly to illustrate the most commonly used categories. Designations such as "express cruiser," "center console," and "convertible" are convenient, though each of these embraces a substantial variety of sizes and configurations. Each boat pictured here is a good one, but not all the good ones are pictured. Far from it. Limitations of space and the availability of good black-and-white photographs were primary considerations.

Runabouts

Runabouts are the essence of speedboating; they exist solely for the purpose of having a good time on the water. You can't really fish from them, and though some have a small enclosed area forward, most runabouts offer little in the way of shelter or other amenities, so they aren't well suited to cruising, either. But they are fun!

You can ski behind most of them, but serious skiers usually demand the kind of dedicated performance—flat wake, towing pylon, etc.—offered by boats such as the Mastercraft. The downside to a pure ski boat is that its hull shape doesn't take to rough water, so the best ski boats are really suited only for skiing.

Runabouts have been popular since the earliest days of powerboating. The Chris-Craft shown here is a limited-edition reproduction—in real mahogany, but built with modern technology for longer life and lower maintenance—of a boat that was built in 1930. The Packard also recalls that era, but in a fiberglass version. The other models shown reflect contemporary ideas in styling. Though the appearance has changed, the fun hasn't.

The Cobalt 252 Condurre typifies the "bowrider" form, open at the bow, which came on the scene in the mid 1960s and is popular because it creates more usable space—especially important when the boat is small to begin with. The lack of a covered foredeck does make a bowrider more susceptible to taking on water

when seas kick up, but runabouts are meant mostly for fair weather.

Runabouts are often offered in packages that include boat, motor, trailer, and all necessary accessories. Volume buying on the part of the manufacturers allows you to buy "the package" for less than you'd probably pay if you gathered the individual components yourself.

I've included the Sea Ray Pachanga with the runabouts despite its large forward cabin, because the boat has the sporty feel of a runabout. However, she could also have been put in the cuddy section, or perhaps even among performance boats.

Chris-Craft 24-Foot Mahogany Runabout

Cobalt 252 Condurre

Sea Ray Pachanga 27

Donzi Sweet Sixteen

Packard 2600

Maxum Sixteen Hundred/XR

MasterCraft Tristar 190 Ski Boat

Performance Boats

Performance boats might be considered runabouts on steroids. Boasting hulls that are often derived directly from past or current winners on the racing circuit, they carry a lot of horsepower and may get you where you want to go faster than your car! They are indeed very macho (as more than a couple of the model names would suggest) and are often called "muscleboats." Performance boats are part of the boating scene and can be a lot of fun, but I believe that the skill required to handle them properly takes them out of the "getting started" category. The Scarab photo makes two points: Even muscleboats can be outboard powered, and their fun isn't necessarily limited to going fast!

Aronow 37

Wellcraft 26 Scarab Sprint

Cruisers Inc. 2520 Rogue

Center Consoles

Center consoles are pure fishing boats. No cabin to clutter the deck, no frills to get in the way. Nothing but hull, power plant(s), a place to hang the controls, electronics, and your fishing gear. They are the essence of efficiency.

Center consoles were once used mostly in boats under 25 feet, but that's no longer true. With larger boats has come the option of a fair-sized tower for even greater fishing efficiency.

The center console's simplicity permits little shelter and risks the loss of full support from nonfishing family members, most of whom want some sort of cabin. However, shelter need not be totally lost. The T-Top on the Donzi and the hard tops on the Ocean Master and Hydra-Sports offer protection from the sun and could be rigged with removable side curtains. The Whaler sports fold-down canvas options that are often used on this kind of boat.

Ocean Master 31

Boston Whaler Outrage 25

Hydra-Sports 3300 SF Vector

Donzi F-18

Cuddy Cabins

Their interior accommodations range from a vestigial berth space for catnaps to a "house" with a semblance of a galley and dining area, but the small cabins we call cuddies all have two things in common: They provide shelter—a place to get away from full exposure to weather—and offer privacy—a place where a person can change into or out of a bathing suit, go to the head, or escape the crowd. Because these amenities so enhance the enjoyment of a boat, cuddies in all their forms are very popular.

Many of the models are designated "walk-around," and even some that aren't so named have the feature. The concept, which first saw light of day in the late 1970s, makes possible a fishing boat with most of the advantages of a center console and shelter, too. Side decks around the cabin permit an angler to work a catch no matter what. With the "conventional" cuddy, this is not so.

Cabin space varies with the size and style of the boat. If you want to be able to walk around the cabin, you have to accept that it won't be as roomy as one that extends from gunwale to gunwale.

Pro-Line 280 Walkaround

Boston Whaler 25' Walkaround

Wellcraft 210 Coastal

Sea Ray 260 Overnighter

Pursuit 2550 Cuddy Cabin

Express Cruisers

The model designations give you an inkling of what this style of boat is all about—"Sunbridge, Mid-Cabin, Sundancer." The idea is to have an open cockpit, with the bridge or console area raised slightly, which permits extending the cuddy in several directions. Raising the cockpit, or at least the forward end of it, enables the foredeck to be raised also, and this makes possible a stand-up cabin with a galley and an enclosed head. The space beneath the bridge becomes what is generally known as a mid-cabin. How much of a benefit this is depends greatly on the size of the boat and the cleverness of the designers, but at the very least it offers another berth (even if you have to crawl in and out of it), and in many models—generally from 30 feet up—it really enlarges the saloon both in usable square footage and in effective use, adding more seating and perhaps a cocktail or game table. Raising the bridge has a third benefit: better visibility from the helm.

Given that the area beneath the forward portion of the cockpit is occupied by the mid-cabin, the engine(s) must go farther aft. This means that most raised-bridge, mid-cabin cruisers have either stern drives or V-drives. A few models manage enough room for both the mid-cabin and an engine compartment far enough forward to use conventional underwater running gear, but this is rare in boats less than 36 feet long.

Other features common to the genre include ample benches and seats for lounging and transom doors for better access to the (usually, these days) integral transom platform.

There's one boat in this series that almost doesn't belong: the Blackfin 32 Combi. It's here because, if you were to remove the optional tower, it would look quite similar to the other raised-bridge models. As the tower suggests, this is a die-hard fishing machine, so instead of a mid-cabin beneath the bridge, the engine compartment is there to allow a pure fishing cockpit with its appurtenances (fish boxes, etc.) back aft. The raised bridge does, however, still offer better visibility than a center console as well as the room to expand the forward area from a mere cuddy into a full-blown cabin with a lot more in the way of creature comforts and amenities than you could possibly find in a walkaround.

Blackfin 32 Combi

Sea Tech 45 Express

Sea Ray 350 Sundancer

Slickcraft 279 SC

Wellcraft St. Tropez

Bayliner 2755 Ciera Sunbridge

Convertibles

These are boats with real cabins—fully equipped galleys with stoves and home-like refrigerator/freezer space, enclosed heads with showers, and full-size hanging lockers as big as shoreside closets. In other words, these are boats you can comfortably spend some time aboard. Because they are convertibles, they have fishing cockpits, too: real fishing cockpits, that is, not merely the convenient "back porch" often tagged onto motoryachts.

If any boat comes close to being all things to all people, it is the convertible. There's enough room inside and out for just about any aspect of boating you'd want to consider. The drawback is the size it takes to gain such versatility. Though there are convertibles on the market in the 28-foot range, other boats are more practical in smaller sizes. Thus, the smallest boat I show here is a 37-footer. Likewise, I have seen convertibles much larger than any included here, but I don't believe these represent an entirely practical application of the style.

Convertibles

Tiara 4300

Striker 37 Canyon Runner

Davis 47 Sportfisherman

Viking 53' Convertible

Bertram 37

Flying Bridge (Sedan) Cruisers

Keep the cabin and flying bridge of the convertible and (usually) reduce the cockpit to less than tournament-fishing dimensions and you have the flying bridge cruiser—sometimes called a sedan. It, too, can represent the best of both worlds in that all but the most serious anglers will probably find the cockpit adequate.

In fact, both the Phoenix and the Tiara are listed by the builders as "convertibles." I included them in this section because the photos show how such boats appear when not rigged for fishing. What counts is not what a builder or dealer calls a particular model but rather how the boat is set up. Despite the fishing rods on the Tollycraft, her comparatively small cockpit makes her less a convertible and more a cruiser with "fishability."

Note that the Esprit has a lower profile than the others. The bridge on this boat is not as high as most, and the cabin layout is slightly different, but the bridge is higher than that of most express cruisers, and her overall arrangement makes the boat more of a candidate for this category. One advantage of the design is a lower center of gravity and the ability to carry proportionally more weight on the bridge without becoming topheavy.

Though the Magnum is based on a performance hull, its cabin and flying bridge put it squarely into the flying bridge cruiser category.

Sea Ray 500 Sedan Bridge

Cruisers, Inc. 2970 Espirit

Magnum 53 Flybridge Cruiser

Tollycraft 34' Sport Sedan

Tiara 3600

Carver 28 Mariner/Voyager

Phoenix 33

Motoryachts

The distinction between "cabin cruiser" and "motoryacht" is probably arbitrary, but 40 feet seems a reasonable length at which to draw the line (although I have seen some 36-footers that, by virtue of accommodations and overall style, would seem to qualify for motoryacht status). Perhaps style and intended use, rather than length overall, make this distinction also. The real key is comfort, and that's something you'll find aplenty in each of these boats.

The Tollycraft 44 and Carver 48 are double cabin models; that is, they have a "split level" arrangement with the aft deck directly above the after cabin. From the aft deck you can go up to the bridge or down to the saloon, and from the saloon farther down to both the after and forward cabins. I have used this arrangement to illustrate the semidisplacement hull in Chapter 5 (boat B in Figure 5-1).

There are motoryachts so big that more crew are needed to run them than there are berths on any of the boats shown here. Megayachts (generally defined as those over 90 feet long) are virtually small ships. Such vessels are not the concern of this book (we have generally figured our upper size limit to be about 60 feet).

Although a motoryacht might not seem the ideal candidate for a first boat, many newcomers to the sport have begun with boats of this size simply because they offer accommodations and cruising ranges that smaller boats can't match. It is easier to start smaller and work your way up as your experience grows, but that is not the only way. I've known a number of people who started with big boats and overcame their lack of experience by hiring a professional captain on a part-time basis to give them hands-on training. It works.

Tango 60

Nordic 480

Hatteras 54 Extended Deckhouse Motoryacht

Tollycraft 44 Cockpit Motoryacht

Carver 4839 Cockpit Motoryacht

Trawler Yachts

To the purist, only a working, payload-carrying fish gatherer deserves to be called a trawler. But the term trawler yacht persists. It began in 1962 with a boat dubbed the Grand Banks 36. Partly because of the deep-sea fishing image conjured up by the name, and partly due to the various traditional workboat lines that were amalgamated into the Grand Banks design, the boating public came to call the boat a "trawler," and the appellation stuck. You can see a Grand Banks 46 in Figure 2-1.

Trawlers are excellent for extended cruising and offer a lot of living space in a generally seaworthy hull. Because early models were either

Kady-Krogen 42

full displacement or barely into the semidisplacement mode and were built mostly in the Orient, trawler yachts have sometimes been disparaged as "slow boats from China." These days, however, it is not unusual to see them move a bit faster. The Maine-built Sabreline, for example, has a sprightly semidisplacement hull.

Krogen 36 Manatee

Sabreline 36

Houseboats

Houseboats were once more house than boat and meant for use on only the most protected waters. They still offer much more in the way of interior accommodations foot for foot of overall length than any other type of boat. But while they are still not meant for real offshore cruising, you'll note from the bows of these boats that they are no longer necessarily flat-bottomed "river" boats. Today's houseboats often reflect the marriage of houseboat superstructure and cruiser-like hull. See also Figure 1-3.

Holiday Mansion Coastal Cruiser

Bluewater 48

Other Traditions

"Trawlers" aren't the only workboats to be emulated in the pleasureboat field. Derivatives of tugboats and Downeast lobster boats are also seen. Like the trawlers, these boats offer a "salty" look and the benefits of hull shapes that have been proven through the test of time.

Portsmouth 30

Henrique Maine Coaster 36

Nordic Tug 26

Same Hull, Different Boat

I've included this category to illustrate a point that is often forgotten. Because of the money tied up in tooling—the molds from which the boats are made—builders will often use the same hull mold to produce two or more boats to reach two or more markets. The differences can be as minor as the variations in layout shown here in the Formulas, or marked enough to produce unique boats that happen to share a hull. If you like the way a hull performs but aren't wild about its cabin or cockpit layout, ask about other models with the same hull. Dealers rarely stock every model, and naturally will make an initial attempt to sell what they have rather than risk losing a sale because the customer doesn't want to wait for delivery of an "ordered" boat.

Same Hull, Different Boats

Formula 242 SS

Formula 242 LS

Tiara 3300 Flybridge

Tiara 3300 Open

A

Active systems, antiroll
    devices, 22-23
After-bow spring
    and docking, 128-130
    and leaving dock,
      133-134
Anchors
    anchor rode, 154-155
    CQR anchors, 150-151
    Danforth anchors,
      148-149
    fortress anchors,
      149-150
    Navy-type anchors, 148
    pairs of anchors, use of,
      62-163
    plow anchors, 150-151
    selection process, 147
    setting the anchor,
      158-160
    single-fluke anchors,
      150-151
    size factors, 151-153
    weighing anchor,
      160-162
    windlass and pulpit and,
      156
    yachtsman's anchors,
      147-148
Antiroll devices, 19
    active systems, 22-23
    flopper stoppers, 22
    paravanes, 22
    passive systems, 22

B

Backing up
    side thrust and, 78
    single-screw boats, 108
    transom-powered
      boats, 122

    twin-screw boats,
      115-116
Beam of boats, performance
    and, 46
Boat reviews, use of, 61-64
Bottom of boat,
    performance and, 43
Buoyancy, factors
    affecting, 44, 46
Buying decisions
    accommodations, 4-5
    dealer and, 70-71
    features of boat and,
      9-12
    guidelines for, 65-71
    size factors, 3-4
    uses of boat and, 5-9

C

Catamarans, 29-30
Cathedral hull, 29
Center consoles, types of,
    190
Chine flats, 26-27
Chine walking, 26
Chopper gun method, 33
Cleats, attaching docklines
    to, 144-145
Clutches, splitting clutches,
    80
COMDTINST M16672.2A,
    181
Constant deadrise hulls, 25
Convertibles, types of, 193
Cored laminates, hull
    construction, 31, 33
CQR anchors, 150-151
Crew members, handling
    of, 179-180
Crossing situations,
    handling of, 182-183
Cruising, boat for, 7-8
Cuddy cabins, types of, 191

Current
    effect on powerboats,
      93-94
    gauging current, 100

D

Danforth anchors, 148-149
Dealer and buying boat,
    70-71
Deep draft, stability and,
    20-21
Deep-V hulls, 24-25
DeltaConic hull, 28
Diesel engines, advantages/
    disadvantages of, 52
Discharge screw current,
    74, 80
Displacement hulls
    antiroll devices, 21-24
    performance and, 13
    speed and, 14-17
    stability and, 13-14,
      18-21
Distribution panels, 47
Diving, boat for, 7
Docking
    docklines, 137-146
    single-screw boats,
      102-107
    springlines, 127-137
    transom-powered boats,
      119-122
    twin-screw boats,
      111-119
Docklines, 137-146
    belaying eye to cleat,
      144-145
    chafing gear and,
      141-143
    lines for alongside pier,
      138
    materials/dimensions of
      lines, 139-141

Docklines, *cont.*
    number required, 138
    pilings, attaching to,
        145-146
Drive systems
    diesel engines, 52
    gasoline engines, 50-52
    jet drives, 59
    outboards, 54-55
    single-screw boats, 52-53
    sterndrives, 56-57
    surface piercing, 57-59
    twin-screw boats, 53-54
    V-drives, 54

E

Electrical system, quality
    aspects, 47
Express cruisers, types of,
    192

F

Fender boards, 143
Fenders, 142-143
Fiberglass
    chopper gun method, 33
    hand layup method, 33
    hull construction, 33-34
Fine entry, performance
    and, 43-44
Fishing, boat for, 5-7
Flare, performance and,
    44-45
Floating, boats and, 12-13
Flopper stoppers, 22
Flying bridge cruisers,
    types of, 195
Fortress anchors, 149-150
Forward-bow spring
    and docking, 130-132
    and leaving dock, 134
Freeboard, performance
    and, 46

G

Gasoline engines, advantages/
    disadvantages of, 50-52

Gull wing hull, 29

H

Hand layup method, 33
Hardware, quality aspects,
    49
Horsepower, increasing
    power, effects of, 30-31
Houseboats, types of, 198
Hull performance, 39-50
    beam and, 46
    bottom cleanliness and,
        43
    bow and fine entry,
        43-44
    dimensions of hull and,
        40-43
    displacement hulls and,
        13
    flare and, 44
    freeboard and, 46
    hull depth and, 42
    planing hulls, 30-31
    quality, checkpoints for,
        47-50
Hull speed, 14-15
Hull types
    displacement hulls,
        13-24
    planing hulls, 24-36
    same hull/different
        boats, types of,
        199-200
    semidisplacement hulls,
        37-39
Hydrodynamic lift, 35

I

Inlet running
    difficulties encountered,
        165-166
    pitchpoling and, 169-170
    strategies for, 167-168

J

Jet drives, advantages/
    disadvantages of, 59

K

Kevlar/fiberglass boats, 34

L

Length of boat, speed and,
    15, 17
Life jackets, weather
    problems, 177
Lookout, maintaining
    proper, 181-182
Lower explosive limit, 52

M

Maintenance costs, 67
Meeting situations, handling
    of, 182
Metacentric height, stability
    and, 20
Modified-V hulls, 27-28
Momentum, steering and,
    75-76
Motoryachts, types of, 196

N

Navy-type anchors, 148

O

Outboards, advantages/
    disadvantages of, 54-55
Overtaking situations,
    handling of, 183-184

P

Pads, performance hulls, 27
Paravanes, 22
Partying, boat for, 8-9
Passive systems, antiroll
    devices, 22
Performance boats, types of,
    189
PFDs, 177
Pilings, attaching docklines
    to, 145-146
Pitchpoling, inlet running
    and, 169-170
Planing hulls
    cathedral hull, 29

construction of, 31-33
deep-V hulls, 24-25
DeltaConic hull, 28
fiberglass, 33-34
horsepower of, 30-31
modified-V hulls,
   27-28
trim and stability,
   35-36
weight of, 31
Plastic foams, hull
  construction, 31
Plow anchors, 150-151
Plumbing system, quality
  aspects, 47-48
Pounds-per-inch
  immersion, 40
Power
   disadvantages to adding
    power, 30-31
   speed and, 17
Powerboats
   current and, 93-94
   drive systems, 50-59
   hull performance
    factors, 39-50
   hull types, 13-39
   steering forces, 74-77
   stopping, 77-78
   transom-powered boats,
    83-88
   wind and, 88-92
Powerboat types
   center consoles, 190
   convertibles, 193
   cuddy cabins, 191
   express cruisers, 192
   flying bridge cruisers,
    195
   houseboats, 198
   motoryachts, 196
   performance boats, 189
   runabouts, 187
   trawler yachts, 197
   workboats, 199
Print-through, 33
Pulpit, anchor and, 156

R
Range, factors related to,
  10
Resins, new materials, 34
Righting moment, stability
  and, 20
Rudder, steering and,
  74-75
Rules of the Road
   in crossing situations,
    182-183
   maneuverability and,
    184
   in meeting situations,
    182
   in overtaking situations,
    183-184
   proper lookout, 181-182
Runabouts, types of, 187
Running strakes, 26

S
Safety
   in problem weather,
    172-178
   Rules of the Road,
    181-184
Seaworthiness, factors
  related to, 10, 12
Semidisplacement hulls,
  37-39
Shape of boat, speed and,
  15, 17
Side thrust, 75, 79, 83
   backing up and, 78
   elimination of, 84, 120
   theories of, 75
   trim and, 83-86
Single-fluke anchors,
  150-151
Single-screw boats
   advantages/disadvantages
    of, 52-53
   backing up, 108
   docking of, 102-107
   turning restrictions,
    108-111

understanding behavior
  of, 96
Speed
   displacement hulls,
    14-17
   factors related to, 9
   hull speed, 14-15
   power and, 17
   shape and, 15, 17
   speed-to-length ratios,
    15, 17
Splitting clutches, 80
Springlines, 127-137
   for docking
    after-bow spring,
     128-130
    forward-bow spring,
     130-132
   for leaving berth
    after-bow spring,
     133-134
    forward-quarter
     spring, 134
   quick release and, 135,
    137
Stability
   antiroll devices, 21-24
   displacement hulls,
    13-14, 18-21
   forces related to, 19-20
   trim and planing hulls,
    35-36
Steering boat
   forces related to,
    74-76
   momentum and,
    75-76
   rudder and, 74-75
   twin-screw boats, 79-80
Sterndrives, advantages/
  disadvantages of, 56-57
Stopping boat, 77-78
Storms. See Weather
  problems
Surface piercing,
  advantages/disadvantages
  of, 57-59

T

Trailering, 122-127
Transom-powered boats
  advantages of, 83
  backing up, 122
  docking of, 119-122
  trailering methods, 122-127
  trim and, 83-88
  twin transom-power drives, 88
  understanding behavior of, 98-99
Trawler yachts, types of, 197
Trim
  optimum trim, 86
  side thrust and, 83-86
  stability and, 35-36
  trim drill, 87-88
  trimming the drives, 86-87
Twin-screw boats
  advantages/disadvantages of, 53-54
  advantages of, 54, 79-80
  backing up, 115-116
  counter-rotating props and, 79, 83, 98
  current, effects of, 117
  disadvantages of, 53
  docking of, 111-119
  understanding behavior of, 97-98
  wind, effects of, 116
Twin transom-power drives, 88

V

Variable deadrise hulls, 28
V-drives, advantages/ disadvantages of, 54

W

Warped plane hulls, 28
Waterline plane, 40
Waterskiing, boat for, 8
Watertight integrity, quality aspects, 49
Weather problems
  escaping rough weather, 172-174
  general precautions, 177-178
  heaving to, 176-177
  high ground, staying on, 175-176
  life jackets, use of, 177
  riding out storm, 174-175
  sensing weather, 171
  speed of boat and, 175
Weight, performance and, 31
Wind
  effect on powerboats, 88-92
  gauging wind, 99-100
Windlass, anchor and, 156
Workboats, types of, 199

Y

Yachtsman's anchors, 147-148